Blogging for Beginners, Create a Blog and Earn Income

Best Marketing and Writing Methods You NEED; to Profit as a Blogger for Making Money, Creating Passive Income and to Gain Success RIGHT NOW.

By Michael Nelson & David Ezeanaka

Table of Contents

Introduction: Should You Start a Blog?

The internet has certainly grown in massive proportions when it comes to what we can now do online; from online shopping, watching movies, listening to music, and social media, there are many things that the internet has granted us in our favor.

However, with the rise of the internet world has come a drought in many areas, especially for brick and mortar stores and businesses. With many folks shopping and conducting business online, there is less of a need for a physical world as we embrace a digital realm in the years to come.

How is one to make a living when regular jobs are a dying breed? I am glad you asked!

The rise of the internet has also given the human race the real possibility to make a passive income online by working a fraction of the typical 9-5 job. What does this mean for you? This gives you the opportunity to spend more time with your loved ones while you do what you are passionate about, and not having to worry yourself over paying the bills.

There are many avenues to create a passive income from the comfort of your own home, but one of the cons about the internet is how much false information is out there; it can be overwhelming to anyone, even experienced people.

Within this book, we will discuss all the details on one of the best ways to use your passion(s) to help you create a substantial income: blogging.

Blogging is not becoming popular, it IS popular right now! You may have overheard a neighbor or friend talk about their success with blogging, but this term is quite vague when one is trying to decide what avenue to take in creating another source of income.

Whether you are an internet guru or are a total newbie to the World Wide Web, this book will discuss all the ins and outs to get you started on the path to financial freedom and a life of fulfillment!

Do you have a hobby or interest you want to dabble in and learn more about? Are you passionate about something that you could really engulf yourself in? Then starting a blog is a superb way to engage yourself in these interests while teaching others, creating a community of like-minded people, and creating a side or even full-time income for you and your family.

A few great reasons to start a blog:

- Creating a support system
- Getting readers to hang on your every word
- Make your social media time worthwhile
- Creating relationships from all over the world
- Become an enhanced writer
- Giving yourself the freedom to experience opportunities for free
- Add consistency to your life
- And MANY more!

The information in this book was researched thoroughly to ensure steps and advice are updated for 2018 and beyond. Throw everything you know about blogging away because, Dorothy, we are not in 2010 anymore.

If you are ready to consistently put blood, sweat, and tears into your blogging biz from the very beginning, you have an awesome chance in experiencing success from your efforts!

What are you waiting for? Let's dive in and see what it takes to become a successful blogger!

Chapter 1: Blog Prepping for Success

Now that you know you want to start a blog, it is time to get your hands dirty. You must dust off that lightbulb in your mind to brainstorm, get technical to create a website, learn how to engage people with promotions and advertisements, and learn how to create high-quality content to hook people into your blog before you will see any money rolling into your account.

Please, do not let that first paragraph scare you away from blogging, for it can easily become a hefty asset that you can create with a little know-how and hard work. Thankfully, you don't have to be a technical wizard to create a blogging website to house the value you are bound to add to the lives of your soon-to-be readers.

Before You Even Think about the Tech-Stuff...

Before creating a blog, you need to make some preparations beforehand. Following aspirations is always fun, but without practicing caution, you are bound to experience failure before you even begin.

In this chapter, you will need to learn as much as you can about yourself, what you want to blog about, and other issues that can hold you back in the long-run from achieving success through blogging.

Since most of you are likely total newbies to all this, we have made it simple; just follow along through this step-by-step process to create a strong outline. This will be the base of your blog's foundation. (a.k.a. this is VITAL to your success!)

Who will be your targeted audience?

Your blog's *target audience* is a specific group of individuals that your blog's content, promotions, and advertisements will be aimed towards. In other words, these are the people you are creating your blog for.

Your blog's audience and picking the proper group of people is going to heavily affect everything else you will be figuring out in this book, so it's best we figure it out early.

- Are you going to be appealing to guys who love cars?
- Girls who need help with makeup?
- Parents who want to hear about parenting tips?

The possibilities are almost endless, so it's not as hard of a question to answer as it seems, but before you answer this question yourself, let's ask another important question:

What will be your blog's niche?

Your blog's *niche* is a topic or multiple subjects that are clearly defined and covered by your blog. In other words, your content will be written with a specific audience within in a specific niche.

Finding the proper niche is not only one of the most challenging decisions of a blogger, but one of the most crucial. If your focus is too broad, you will fail to appeal to anyone, which will lead to confusion and failure.

However, if your niche is too focused, or "niched-down", you will have very few people to sell to, which will lead to a lack of traffic, which means not a lot of followers and little to no income for all your efforts. Imagine if your favorite TV show randomly switched genres and characters every couple episodes. I imagine you would be a little peeved, you expect to see the story you were planning on watching.

So, what's the difference between that and a random blog? Not much. Not many people are looking to read a blog that's only about someone's life. As much fun it may be to talk about yourself, most people just aren't going to seek out that content, let alone pay for it in some way. We should find a more realistic topic, something that can appeal to people, and be fun to read/write about.

Picking your blog's niche:

- What do you enjoy writing about? If you have a passion for gardening, it feels almost natural to start a blog about your garden. Do you love talking with your friends about music? Turn those conversations into blog posts and engage with the online community about your love of music.

- What do you think people might be wanting from a blog? (What's currently missing from the other blogs on the internet?) One of the motivations begin creating a blog could be to fill the space you found in the online community. Maybe you discover there's a major lack of blogs about heavy metal covers of common lullaby's, you could fill in that gap! Just because something is missing, it doesn't mean there is no demand for it.

- What do you know a good amount about? (Cooking, technology, cars, makeup, parenting, etc.) While it's not completely necessary to have a good understanding of a topic you pick, it will definitely help you if you do. If you know almost everything about horror movies, it'd make sense to write about it.

You might have a few worries about picking your topic, and that's okay. Everyone has some problems, but to be honest, it's hard to mess up picking a topic. There are no wrong topics, you don't need to be extremely educated on the topic, and you don't even have to stick to one topic specifically. Let's delve a little bit deeper into some common excuses.

One worry you might have is that you might pick an unpopular topic for your blog. The truth is there are no wrong answers when picking a topic. Even if you pick the most off the wall topic, you will still be able to build an audience. It might even help you if you pick an uncommon blog topic, you could build an audience for a topic that wasn't expected to be as popular as it is.

Don't be afraid to pick an uncommon topic, if you have passion for the blog, it will grow. However, if worse comes to worse, and you realize you don't like the topic you chose, that's okay. No one is forcing you to write about something you don't enjoy writing about. There are many ways to get out of a topic.

One way is to slowly change to another idea. If you started writing about music, but realized that you enjoy writing about movies more, you can slowly alter until you're only writing about movies. If you lose some readers because of the topic change, that's fine, don't panic. There's no reason to continue blogging about uninteresting things, it will only lead to burnout.

What if you have far too many interests to pick only one? That's okay, you don't need to stick to only one topic! While I do highly recommend that you only stick to a couple topics, that are at least correlated in some way, you don't necessarily need to only write about one idea. Let's say my imaginary blog is going to be about technology. That is a pretty broad topic, so we'll whittle it down a little bit to make it more precise.

Let's say I want to make a blog about video games, a topic I know a little bit about. I could also probably get away with writing about game consoles too, and could even possibly write about something almost unrelated, like music. Another way you could merge topics is make it a gimmick of the posts. A blog that is self-aware of how the two topics they write about are completely unrelated could work. A blog about fishing and kitchen tips could work.

Take notice that I said I know a small amount about video games, because I'm definitely no expert. I play less than a few hours a week, and only sort of keep up with the game news. You might also feel the same way about a topic. You may dabble in something and are unsure if you should pursue the topic because of your lack of experience.

There are very many ways around this, one of which is to be honest with the readers. Admit to them that you created the blog to learn more about your topic. Another way around is to start with more opinionated ideas. If I know nothing about games, I could start with some game reviews. Opinions cannot be wrong, so you should have no fear of inexperience.

Hopefully you have found a topic that you're willing to give a shot at. As my example, I will be using video games as my topic for my example blog.

Creation of the *ideal* reader

You will need to figure out what the demographics of your readers are, so the content you create can be tailored towards them. The more your writing appeals to your ideal reader, the more traction your blog will gain. If I'm writing about video games, I must generalize the people who play video games. Typically, they are younger than 30 or 40, most are probably attending school in some form, and most are probably familiar with the internet and technology. Take a second to think about your topic's ideal reader.

Let's get a little bit more specific about relating to your readers. While it would be nice to have a blog that appeals to everyone, it's unrealistic. You need to understand your *ideal* reader. This is a personification of what you expect your most common audience to be like. We need to get loyal readers to the blog because loyal readers are the most likely to become customers, which are crucial if you plan on making a profit from your blog. So, let's figure out some of our ideal readers.

Reader Personality

One thing we need to consider is our ideal reader's personality. What are some of their hobbies, where do they live, what are they doing with their friends, what sites do they use online, what social media platforms do they use? We don't need to answer all these questions immediately, but we should try to get a rough outline done before starting our writing. If I'm trying to appeal to people who play video games, I need to consider my demographic once again. They are most likely on the younger side, so that also implies they might be in school or college.

This means that they might not put in as much time into games as someone without classes and studying to worry about. If they play video games, and are reading my blog, that must mean they are familiar with technology and the internet. With these three factors, we can move forward to their internet presence.

Reader's Habits on Social Media

If they found your blog, they most likely know how to navigate on the internet. That must also mean that they are at least aware of social media (who isn't these days?), so they might have a social media presence. We must think for a moment and wonder what kind of social media websites they use.

Each website has an understandable demographic, if you follow the front page of said social media website. Here a just a couple of examples of what I think my ideal reader would use:

- *Facebook*: The most popular social media site by far, Facebook gets over 5 billion daily views! With these ridiculous numbers, Facebook is like the free space in bingo. Advertising on Facebook is free, easy, and gets viewed by as many people as you have the time to add.

- *Reddit*: Reddit has a little bit of everything for everyone, meaning that it's easy to find people who not only share common interests, but also have tips for fellow bloggers. Following and linking your blog in the subreddits that relate to your topic can very easily drive blog views up.

- *YouTube*: YouTube is one of the most popular streaming services available, and it's completely free to upload to and view. Making a small channel that explains your blogs and maybe even uploading a couple video format blogs would help growth. Many younger people use YouTube for entertainment, so it could be very beneficial to use that website to promote my game blog.

- *Snapchat*: While Snapchat is very popular amongst younger people, it pretty much stops there. Of course, there are examples of all demographics on Snapchat, the majority happen to be in school and are young. While it may not work for you specifically, it definitely works for my demographic.

- *Twitter*: Lots of people use Twitter, and many companies have official Twitter pages, which raises the site's credibility. Making an official Twitter for your blog will help its outreach, which is one of our main goals. You could even start your own hashtags and promote your blog. Lots of people in school use Twitter, so this definitely fits my demographic.

Another thing to practice is cross-promotion amongst your social media accounts. Make sure to include a link to your Twitter page on Facebook, upload your snap code to your Twitter, and always include a link to the website hosting your blog, (We'll get to website creation later).

Financial Habits of the Ideal Reader

Now, because we plan on profiting from this blog, we need to consider the economics of our ideal reader. A few questions to ask are:

How does the age demographic use money? Do they save up every cent they can, or do they spend all their paycheck recklessly? Are they willing to donate their money to content they enjoy, or do they expect a product in return for their charity? We'll get into profiting from products and donations later, but these are still things you should consider before moving onwards.

So, what if we run into a problem with relating to our ideal reader? What if my audience is full of people I didn't expect to read my content? What if every single one of my guesses about my reader is wrong? Then I change it. Of course, you are going to have to adjust your view of your ideal reader, you're no psychic.

Creating the right persona takes time

I might have accidently assumed that all my readers are in school, but through research of my audience, I find that most are out of school and working part time jobs instead. That's fine, we can adjust, and we will always need to adjust to keep our blogs moving. Running into this problem is far from a death sentence for your blog, it's just as simple as re-imagining your ideal reader.

Let's talk about our personalities. I want to write for people obsessed with video games, but I'm just not that kind of person. We need to relate with our reader, so what do we do in this hopefully rare situation? We'll create a dedicated image of the writer. I may not be a hardcore gamer, but I can hopefully emulate how a hardcore gamer writes. Research the lingo, study other blogs that are written by actual hardcore gamers, and act like you belong. If you practice these three, you'll relate to your readers in no time.

So now that we know what our blog will be about, what our audience is, what our ideal reader looks like, and what social media to advertise on, it's time to create our blog, or at least get a rough draft of it in our heads.

Chapter 2: Creating & Maintaining Your Blog

So, we have so far:

- Our blog's topic or niche
- An idea of who our ideal reader will be

With a solid outline, you might be feeling very confident. But when it comes to sitting down and turning that outline into a reality, what the heck is next?

Please, forego the Google search; you are naturally going to hear hundreds of answers, from hundreds of people, all telling you what you need to do first. The thing is, there is no definite answer. You will be sucked into the world of YouTube tutorials and endless long-form posts.

However, there is a good and proven route to take to ensure that your blog can be as successful as possible and there's a good route to take if you want to be as successful as possible. That's the route we're going to take, so we can ensure this blog works out with the end goal of beginning to earn a profit from our blogging efforts.

Takes money to make money!

Speaking of profits, there is a disclaimer I should go ahead and get out of the way; you are going to have to give a little to get a little. It will cost you some money up front to get started building your dream blog; this is just a fact when it comes to the reality of the online world.

Yes, you could technically let a website host your blog for free, but that's not a step we should take if we plan on truly making this blog our own. We're going to have to shell out some investment money into a domain and hosting site just to get started. That is an intimidating process, but we'll walk through that together as well.

Purchasing a Domain

So, what is a domain? To put it simply, it's the name of the website you type into the URL bar to get to a website. An example is *www.Facebook.com*. It should be relatively short, easy to spell, and professional. Depending on your demographic, you should try to avoid slang, misspellings, and overly complicated or hard to spell words. Get a concrete idea in your head of what you would like your domain to be. I'm going to say mine will be, *www.MyGamingBlog.com*.

First, we will need to see if this domain is available to purchase. There are many websites that you can do this on, but one that is favored by myself and many others is *www.GoDaddy.com*.

When I type in the domain I hope to use, I get the result that it's available for purchase, but it's far from my price range, topping off at almost $2300. Luckily, the website offers cheaper variations of the domain, just with different spellings or words. The website tells me that *www.MyGamingBlogs.com* is available, and only $18 for two whole years of ownership, after which I will have to renew my ownership.

This is a much more manageable price than the previous offer. Always look at the alternatives, even if you got a reasonable price for your original domain, you might find something cheaper, or even a name you enjoy more than your current idea.

Naming Your Blog

While the domain and blog name don't have to match, it would probably help if you kept them to the same brand. I will be coming up with name different from my domain in case you chose to do this as well. So, on my website, *www.mygamingblogs.com,* I will be hosting a blog that has a different title than my URL.

This is really where you can let your creativity shine, there are no wrong answers. I want people to feel comfortable reading my blog, I don't want them to feel like they're in over their heads. I don't want it to only cater to a certain group of people who would get an obscure reference. I want anyone reading the name of my blog to feel welcomed, even if they don't play video games. I'll call mine *The Gamer's Den.* It's short, simple, and easy to remember, which are three great characteristics to a name.

Picking a Hosting Plan

So, my domain is purchased, I know what my blog will be called, I need to find a reputable place that will host my newfound blog. Without a host, no one will be able to visit and read anything on your site. It makes all the links, coding and files viewable to the public.

This is not a step you should cheap out on, because without a good host, your website could face many problems such as downtime, login troubles, and slow load times. These are all things that work against your blog. You know those times when a website is extremely slow and keeps giving you error messages, even when you know your WiFi is fine? That is a common issue with the website's host, which makes visitors want to click off the website rather than stay around.

Hosting Site Features to Consider

- Speed
- Features
- Security
- Strong track record
- Type of server
  - Shared hosting
  - VPS hosting
  - Dedicated hosting
  - Cloud Hosting

There are many reliable and affordable hosting services out there to get your blog started. Here are a few that I recommend checking out in 2018:

- *Wordpress.com* – Wordpress.com is the largest community for bloggers on the entire web. Hosted on the WP server, it is easy for beginners to set up. They offer upgrades for small fees and you can upgrade to Wordpress.org anytime.

- *Wordpress.org* – I struggled and had to figure this out for the hard way on my own, but Wordpress.COM and Wordpress.ORG are different entities under the same umbrella. The .org version is essentially the BIG brother of wordpress.com. It is easy to install, and you won't have to be a coder to personalize, but you will be required to have your own domain and hosting.

- *HostGator* – This hosting company is one that likes to keep their costs low for new and experienced bloggers. With a high-quality server, it is fast and very secure. If you have any issues, they also offer 24/7 support.

- *Blogger* – Blogger has been a hosting platform around for a long time and people love the additions to using it. With unique widgets and integrations, there is a lot to like but it is not the best for beginners.

- *Weebly* – Weebly is one of my personal favorites with its drag and drop interface, it is easy to create an entire blog in a matter of an hour. You can start free and upgrade later.

- *Wix* – Wix is like Weebly thanks to its drag and drop features and awesome ready-to-use templates. This is another site where you can start for free and upgrade to a paid version later.

Blog Privacy

Age is the new currency thanks to today's internet advances. Data of any kind, even your blog, can be used against you if the right people get a hold of it. Creating a blog opens the door for hackers to come in, which is why adding privacy should be a priority.

Hackers can gain access to your financial and personal information that is needed for hosting and domain websites to start your blog. It is just enough for your identity to be whisked away and open up credit in your name, ruining that perfect 800+ credit score.

And even if you blog anonymously, there are people that could figure you out and use your blog against you. For instance, if you mention any details about your job, you could be at risk for disciplinary action at the work place. This is just one example.

To keep your data secure as a blogger:

- *Get a PO Box* so that you have a mailing address that is separate from where you reside. This erases the possibility of strangers knowing where you live.

- *ALWAYS click the "domain privacy" option when* you are signing up your domain online. It is a small fee, but it is better to pay $10-12 to ensure your information is safe.

- *Sign-up for a Google Voice Number* to keep your personal number separate from everything business related.

- *Use unique passwords* for every site you use. Yes, this seems like a hassle, but if a hacker figures out one password, they can work their way through your accounts and destroy your life quickly. Also, I highly recommend changing those passwords at least once every 3-6 months to ensure security.

- *Be wary of what you blog about.* Never include specific details, locations, or names of your loved ones. When you share details, fudge them a bit by changes times, locations, names, and dates.

First Year of Blog Costs

- Domain: $15
- Web hosting: $110/year
- Blog theme (optional): $60-90
- Email Marketing Services: $29/month
- Social Media Tools (optional): $10-30/month
- Investing in blogging courses (optional): $49-$1000+

To just get started with a domain and hosting, the average blog without all the fancy themes, media tools, and email services is around $125 per year. However, I would recommend setting up an email marketing service so that you can gather your audience's emails to market to them later on, so a good estimate would be $150 per year. Not bad for a business that could potentially make you 6-figures and up if done properly!

Content Management Systems: WordPress

A *content management system*, or *CMS*, is simply a piece of software that helps you facilitate the creation, editing, organization, and publishing of your content. WordPress is a great CMS, since it allows you to do all these things to get your content out there for eyes to view.

Those that use WordPress have total control over their files and documents, as well as the design and display of their content. You do not need to be an expert coder to publish on this platform. The beauty of a great CMS is that any user can create and manage their content without very much technical know-how.

Selecting a Theme

A blog theme is software that allows you more room to customize your blog's design and appearance, such as fonts, colors, and structure. Especially as a beginner, you will need to choose a newbie-friendly theme. This will save you many headaches, wasted hours, and money as you get your blog up and running.

Most blogging platforms have beautiful free themes already built in that you can use. I suggest that you pick a free theme you like as you first start out and become accustomed to your platform, whether it be WordPress, Weebly, etc.

However, for those that decide to use WordPress, there are two themes I highly recommend:

- *The Divi Theme* is the most popular WP theme on the market and it is suited for beginners. It is $89/year, however. But there are over 70 themes to choose from and customize.

- *The Avada Theme* is another theme software that is suited for beginning bloggers, but it comes in at a lower price of just $60 and the best part about this price is that you only pay it ONE time. The downside that you only get one theme. But if you are wanting to customize your blog more on a budget, I recommend it.

Mobile-Responsive Design

Most of the world is attached to their mobile devices, whether it is their smartphones, tablets, laptops, etc. A website that is responsive simply means that its layout responds and adapts to the size of the screen that someone is looking at it on. This means it automatically changes to the screen so that the user can have ease of access to the website, no matter what device they are looking at it on.

Why should you care about this as a beginner? Because you want your readers to have a great experience on your website so that they will keep coming back to read more!

There are two main things you can do to ensure your blog stays optimized for all your fans:

1. Optimize your content's layout
2. Adapt the content that is shown to readers

Needed Plugins for Your Blog

Did you know that almost a quarter of the entire internet is powered by WordPress? That is A LOT of digital real estate for one platform to cover! With so many people like you thinking about starting a blog and leaning towards WordPress to build their website and make it sustainable, there are more essentials being added to WP's bucket of choices for bloggers to use.

Plug-ins come in handy on blogs and websites. These little guys are not so little, for they are additions that add spunk and functionality to your blog. In this section, I will talk about two sets of plugins: the most downloaded in 2018 so far and ones I personally use and love.

Most Downloaded Free WP Plugins:

- *Akismet* fends off comment spams and even deletes junk comments on your website.

- *Google XML Sitemaps* helps Google to crawl and read through your blog, which allows your website to rank higher for potential users to find it.

- *Contact Form 7* allows beginning and experienced bloggers to forego the effort of creating a content page. It also adds information into posts and allows you to customize forms and drop-down menus.

- *Jetpack* is an umbrella that has more than 30 modules that can help you run a tighter ship of a blog.

- *WooCommerce* is a plugin centered around making e-commerce on your blog easier. It helps bloggers integrate online stores into their content.

- *Wordfence Security* is another level of security above the passwords you already have. It features the ability to block malicious networks and scans for possible vulnerabilities.

- *Yoast SEO* allows all bloggers to get a reign over their SEO (search engine optimization) efforts. SEO in the giant world of online content is critical if you ever want your blog to see the light of day by more than a few people. This plugin assists you in ensuring your content is optimized to its fullest potential.

- *Regenerate Thumbnails* help you to trash blurry images and create media that is pleasing to the eye.

- *WP Super Cache* helps your blog cache, which helps you to install, activate, and configure your setup process and future maintenance more efficiently.

- *Google Analytics by Yoast* saves the need to open extra tabs on your browser so that you can look at your blog's analytics right on the WP dashboard.

WP Plugins I Use and LOVE

- *All 404 Redirect to Homepage* is a simple addition to my blog that helps to redirect any 404 pages back to the homepage.

- *Antispam by CleanTalk* is similar to *Akismet*, but I prefer this plugin since it performs better than the other, and it's just $5/month.

- *Simple Social Share* adds social buttons for people to share my content on their own websites and social media accounts.

- *Scroll Triggered Box* helps my readers pick what newsletters they want in their inboxes from my website.

- *Easy Facebook Like Box* is something that I easily added to my blog. This is a great plugin if you have a dedicated Facebook community centered around your niche and helps readers to share your content straight to the Facebook platform.

- *WP-Polls* helps me to easily create polls for my readers so that I can get an idea of future content to curate.

- *Author Bio Box* is a good plugin to have if your blog or website has multiple folks that help maintain it. It creates special boxes below posts that provide your readers with information about the author and links to their social media profiles.

Useful Blog Widgets

One of the best aspects of WordPress is that it has a huge variety of widgets to help you create and customize your blog. There are many WP themes and plugins that allow you to use various types of widgets such as email subscribe, calendar, etc.

Here are some of the most useful widgets for WP to ensure you are organized and ready to make your blog a success:

- *Recent Posts Widget* is a default WP widget which displays your most recent posts.

- *Category Posts* displays recent posts in a selected category.

- *Simple Social Icons* allows you to set up social media icons directly on the sidebar of your blog.

- *Google Maps* is an easy way for you to add your location to your website. This is especially helpful if you are creating a blog around your online or physical business.

- *Social Count Plus* allows bloggers to display their social media follower count for each of their platforms on the sidebar of their website.

- *Image Widget* allows bloggers to add images to their sidebar without having to write in HTML coding by themselves.

Pages Vs. Posts

WordPress provides users with two ways to create content by default: with posts and pages. To ensure that you have a user-friendly blog, it is crucial that you know the difference between the two.

WordPress posts are labeled with an official publish date and are displayed by the date's order on your blog's page.

When you create a post, you have options to assign it by tags and categories. Both of these help you to organize posts and make it easier for readers to find content on your blog that they are interested in.

WordPress pages do not have a published date displayed are meant more for timeless, static content. Two common examples are "about" and "contact" pages.

Unlike posts, you are not able to use tags or categories on pages. Rather, they are organized hierarchically; that giant word simply means that you can make one page a "parent" and another a "child" page, which allows you to group related pages together cohesively.

Why does knowing the difference between posts and pages matter? Well, it doesn't make any sense to list your content by the date since you want your viewers to always be able to read it, no matter when they take a trip around your blog.

Now that you know all the technical aspects that go into creating a functional blog, it is time to make it look as great as possible so that it will attract more visitors!

Chapter 3: Creating a Professional Looking Blog

Congrats! You are making your way through this book swiftly and gaining the knowledge you need to create a successful and profitable blog! In this chapter, we will discuss how to create and maintain a great looking professional blog that your readers will want to visit time and time again.

Why Consistency is Key in Web Design

In design, consistency is one of the golden rules. To ensure that your readers experience quality when they stop by your blog, you need to be consistent when it comes to the design and the content. (Content consistency will be discussed in Chapter 5). In fact, being consistent is one of the most critical factors that will separate negative and positive experiences users will have on your website.

Consistency involves two crucial factors:

1. Uniformity that is harmonious
2. Coherence and accordance that is logical

Think of it this way: You just prepared a tasty meal in the kitchen located in your home. You open your cutlery drawer to get a knife and fork and start to enjoy your meal. It took you mere seconds to locate eating utensils because you knew where they were instinctively; it was in the same place as last week and the weeks before that.

This is a simple analogy that should also be used in designing your blogging website. Just because *you* know where the content you create is located on the site, does not mean that your readers will be able to quickly find it. Consistency on your blog that is familiar to users who surf other websites will make it more navigable. Users should always be able to find necessary information effortlessly.

Areas where you need to make your blog consistent:

- Website *elements* are the building blocks of your website. They include navigation bars, sidebars, headers, footer, and other patterns.

- *Design* should be consistent, especially the tiny details, which many beginning bloggers overlook. Users will associate certain colors to links and will quickly be able to recognize your website's copy and more.

- Your website's *content* should certainly be consistent, from the tone, mood, quality, and quantity and everything in between. Readers will become familiar with your content's consistency over time. If the design of your website is laid back in nature, your content should match that.

- Your blog's *interaction* should also be consistent. All your users will pick who to interact with on your website in different ways, but the way your blog responds to those interactions should be the exact same.

Consistency is key for any business, but especially for the online real estate simply because users should feel at ease and comfortable using and visiting your website. The way it is designed, arranged, and loaded with valuable content is how they distinguish between your blog and others that are poorly designed.

Creating Categories

One of the biggest mistakes I have made over the years of setting up and designing various blogs was the overuse of labels and categories. These two aspects are valuable tools to all bloggers.

Categories in WordPress are a post organization system where you use keywords to organize your content. They are hierarchical, which means there are levels of organization within categories, which are subcategories. Subcategories are great tools that allow bloggers to break down their larger pieces of content into different sections.

For instance, if you blog about food, one of your Parent categories, or main categories, may be Breakfast, Lunch, and Dinner. Subcategories would be Mexican, German, Italian, etc.

Labels, however, refer to post categorization systems used on websites such as Blogger or BlogSpot. Blogger labels are not hierarchical without Parent or Child labels.

Both Blogger and WordPress allow users to integrate labels and categories into their blogs in many ways. For instance, adding labels and categories in single posts is a superb way to encourage your readers to stick around your website by looking at other posts related to what they have already read.

For instance, readers that find your Green Chile Tamales recipe on your blog after searching Google will likely enjoy other recipes that are categorized under Mexican recipes.

Brainstorming Post Topics

As you will soon learn, brainstorming possible topics to create content for your blog around is one of the difficult aspects of maintaining a successful blog. Finding good topics to write about is harder than it sounds. There are thousands of articles that get published every day, but each only receives a couple hundred likes and shares.

Why is this? Because the content is just not intriguing enough. If you are writing about a dull topic, use visuals to increase popularity. If you find an interesting topic that will intrigue readers, however, your rates of clicks will skyrocket.

How do you brainstorm topics that will interest your blog's readers and how can you determine that those topics will be what you want to read about? Here are some great ideas to get your brainstorming jumpstarted!

- Keep an open mind! Instead of forcing yourself to get into a structured thinking session, consciously stay open to ideas 24/7. When you're just doing average things, ideas are likely to pop into your head more readily.

- Who said you had to brainstorm by yourself? Your friends, family, co-workers, and potential target audience know the interests of your audience. They may have an idea of what will resonate the best.

- Simply type phrases and keywords into the Google search bar to discover amazing topics and ideas! Google will display many ideas right underneath what you type.

- Get input from your readers/customers, because who better to ask than the very people that read your blog and want to do business with you?

  - Speak to readers via email, social media, phone, or in person.
  - Ask questions in social media groups and invite followers to leave comments and questions.
- If you ever list FAQs (frequently asked questions) on your blog, this can be a treasure chest of ideas that you can mine from. Diving into these subjects covered in FAQs means you can give your audience valuable content and improve your SEO results.

SEO Basics

Organic searches online make up more than a third of the traffic that goes to blogs and websites. That is more than paid traffic and social media traffic combined. SEO (search engine optimization) is as relevant as ever. Whether you own your own business, are in marketing, or write blogs, you know that SEO is vital to your success.

Unfortunately, successful SEO requires you to have some extensive knowledge of how search engines functions. Why? Because algorithms are being updated constantly, as much as 500 times *per year*. Yup, thanks Google!

Don't fear; if you learn the foundation of proper SEO practices, you can run out of the gate winning and worry about the mind-boggling metrics when you become more experienced. Here are some of the basics to get you started on the right foot:

- *Links* are important so that your search result comes up within the "3-Pack" on Google; those businesses and websites that show up first! Backlinks are as reliable as old friends, meaning the more people that vouch for your website, the more trustworthy your site will seem to newcomers.

- *Content* is very important and if you neglect its importance to your success, you are doing the entire blogging process incorrectly. Google wants websites to create content that provides value to readers. Also, it looks for consistency and activeness. Content is what keeps people on your website.

  o Create long-form content
  o Create various kinds of content
  o Recycle old content

- Using *headlines and meta descriptions* wisely is crucial, for it is the first thing people see when you come up in the search results. View these as your first impressions. Of course, you want it to be a good first impression!
  o Add keywords close to the beginning
  o Make headlines catchy so people want to click them

- The *user experience* of a website is another aspect that Google collects data on, which is essentially how visitors behave on your blog. Sadly, if your page fails to load fast enough or doesn't have relevant information that viewers are looking for.

  o Increase your site's speed
  o Keep the design clean and simplistic
  o Limit your number of ads

- *Mobile SEO* is more crucial than ever in 2018 and for many decades to come. Google will very soon be looking at the website's mobile speed as a factor for ranking.

  - Optimize your local SEO, meaning you need to think about how your target audience searches for information on their mobile devices.
  - Optimize your site for voice searching
  - Don't hide content by displaying it differently than on desktop view.

Importance of Keyword Research

Effective marketing tools are more readily available now than ever. This means the birth of more opportunities to reach a larger potential market than any brick and mortar business would using traditional methods of marketing.

If you need information on anything, almost everyone these days relies on search engines and the websites that show up. To create a blog that is successful, you will need to get higher in the rankings on search engines so that your website comes up as an option for people to click on. How do you do this?

Well, one of the best ways is by conducting keyword research. Keywords are crucial in helping your blog's content match up to targeted viewers and researches. The more traffic you have to your blog means more paying consumers and money in your bank account.

Basics of keyword research for beginners:

- *Creating a list of keywords* helps you to fill your blog with great content by allowing you to put your feet into your visitors' shoes. This list should consist of intelligent hunches or what people will assume what to look for how your website. View it as the "how, what, where, why, and other queries your visitors might use."

- Streamline your keyword research by *using keyword tools*. There are a large variety of both free and paid tools that can help you get a good idea of great keywords to lead traffic to your blog.

- *Refine your keyword list* by using keyword suggestion tools. These help you to further narrow down your list and write down better insights on how your targeted audience arrange, add, and subtract words from their searches.

- *Be wary using broad keywords.* Don't become one of the many bloggers that use broad words like they are going out of style. Using too many of these will not bring in the traffic you think it will. Use specific words and phrases that will attract lower search volumes instead.

- *Use keyword research for products or services you offer.* Your website might be under various categories, which means you should conduct research for each of those classifications.

- *Maximize long tail keywords.* These don't have a bunch of searches, but those that are performing well on these searches means that they are likely solving very specific issues. Long tail keywords have specific intents and will yield you steady traffic.

Keyword Research Using Pinterest

One of my favorite ways to conduct research on possible keywords for newly created blogs is using Pinterest. Anyone trying to sell or educate people on anything really shouldn't ignore Pinterest. It heavily competes with Google and is the number one visual search engine in the world. Here are ways to utilize Pinterest to ensure your keywords are great for getting traffic to your blog:

- *Explore topics* by searching through popular categories first. Read specific details about their popularity of categories and subcategories. For instance, when you search 'technology', you will see a list of subcategories. When you click on the sub 'virtual reality', you will see a brand-new list of related topics. Each subtopic will provide ideas of valuable topic ideas.

- *Use quick search*; it is like Google, allowing you to view popular phrases with keywords that appear automatically.

- *Use the guided search* by choosing a keyword from quick search and clicking on 'guides' below the search box. Common search terms related to your search will appear.

- *Research with promoted pins* is very similar to researching keywords on Facebook Ads and AdWords. It allows you to use the promoted pins platform to discover keywords and long tail phrases.

- *Test your keywords on Pinterest* before you use them on your blog. Test your keyword strategy by incorporating them on board descriptions, titles, and captions. You can use Pinterest to see how they words perform.

Finding Your Angle

One of the cons of starting a blog in 2018 is that you have *A LOT* of information to sift through, and so does your potential audience. There is so much fluffy intel on the internet that it's not only difficult to be found among the crowd, but it can be challenging to stand out.

Therefore, finding a unique angle and sticking to it is *vital* to your blogging success. It can be tricky to translate raw ideas into angles for posts that people will *want* to read. Here are some methods to find your blog content's angle:

- *Solving a problem* content has great potential because there are always issues to be solved. These posts are very shareable, especially if you are one of the first in your niche to solve and thoroughly explain solutions.

- *How-to* posts perform well for almost every blogger because readers enjoy reading philosophical discussions and debates that kick their brains into overdrive.

- *FAQ* posts provide common answers to questions that readers have, which means that your content will be referred to on a consistent basis.

- *Excerpt* posts take a vital piece of long form content and repurpose it for another piece of content for your blog. For instance, if you have previously written an eBook, find a section that can stand on its own and republish it to your blog as a single post.

- *Comparison* posts are great for comparing products to help your readers make a buying decision easier.

- *Research reveal* posts help you to reveal research you have conducted as a blogger for your website to readers in an entertaining way.

Anatomy of a Good Headline

The job of a headline is to grab the attention of readers and compel them to read your posts thoroughly. You don't need to be an expert writer to curate eye-catching headlines! Here are a few great examples to get you started:

- [Irresistible headline]: Subheading

    - *"The Reason Your Headlines Are Boring Your Audience: Here's How to Revive Them"*

- Here is a Method That is Helping [Blank] to [Blank]

    - *"Here's a Formula That is Helping Brand New Bloggers to Create Click-Worthy Headlines"*

- Little Know Ways to [Blank]

    - *"Little Known Ways to Compel Readers to Continue Reading"*

- SEO Headline

    - *"Effective Headline Writing Tips That Will Get Your Blogs More Readers"*

- Now You Can Have [Something Desirable] [Great outcome]

- *"Now You Can Have Your Readers Raving About Your Blog and Watch It Go Viral!"*

- What Everyone Should Know About [Blank]

  - *"What Everyone Should Know About Writing a Killer Headline"*

- Who Else Wants [Blank]?

  - *"Who Else Wants to Write Clickable Headlines?"*

Content Calendar for Writing

One of the biggest hurdles I had to jump over in building my online business was getting into the proper business-like mindset. I am a great writer, but with all the content I needed to get out onto my blog, I was losing ideas to the air left and right, forgetting my ideas and when to post. Creating a content calendar for my blog was a definite life-saver.

A content calendar is a simple tool used to detail your content and business out for you to see and provides you adequate organization and the ability to stick to your blogging goals.

To build a good content calendar:

1. Brainstorm content that will fit into your niche and persona
2. Create a calendar from 1 to 6 months into the future
3. Test out your content before adding it to the calendar
4. Keep an eye on your blog's surroundings

There are many blogging content calendars out there to ensure that you can keep level-headed as you curate content and brainstorm how to attract your target audience. This is an essential tool for all beginning bloggers.

Here are a couple of my calendar suggestions:

- <u>Free templates</u>
- Paid: <u>CoSchedule</u>

Yes, taking the additional steps to ensure that your new blog comes off as professional to newcomers can certainly be a bit taxing. However, when it comes to the prosperity and successfulness of your blossoming blog, it will be worth all the time and money spent!

Chapter 4: The Nitty-Gritty of Website Creation

Now that you have learned what it takes to discover your niche, gain a piece of internet real estate and create the foundation for a successful and professional blog, you are now prepared to learn all about the pieces that are needed to make your growing blog business a legitimate website.

The About Us Page

The *About Us* page is one of the first pages that new and existing viewers will see when they cross over the threshold of your website. In fact, according to a study conducted in 2018, 16% of visitors check out the About Us page, 33% browse it before going elsewhere on the site, and 47% make a quick trip right to the products and services page.

What does this mean? That 16 out of 100 visitors are interested in learning more about your blog and personal brand. Therefore, you need to beef up your *About Us* page while still making it short, sweet, and to the point. Here are some tips to create a bomb *About Us* page:

- Use a conversational tone to make it warm and friendly.

- Learn how to craft a good story and don't make it a history lesson. Most folks could care less about the overall history of your blog.

- Make this page visually exciting.

- Allow your visitors to do some of the talking for you by adding testimonials.

- Pick only one call to action.

Contact Page

Most blogs have a contact page, as many of you are aware. It is another one of the first pages that you should create when you first begin building your blog. It is very simple on most blogging platforms to add a simple form on your contact page.

Once you begin gaining the interest of many viewers, it can become difficult to maintain the large numbers of emails that enter your inbox from your fans. This can drastically burden your time. So, you need to set up an efficient contact page right from the get-go to save a headache later.

- Set up priorities for incoming emails by creating a personalized drop-down list for emailers to choose from before sending.

- Answer inquiries before they are even asked by identifying the patterns in the requests you receive. I suggest creating a page dedicated to FAQs.

- Make it a priority to review your "reason for contact" drop-down list options and your FAQ page on a regular basis to control the emails you receive.

Legal Requirements for Your Blog

Another big hurdle I overcame as a newbie blogger was figuring out how to create a blog that was legal. Licenses, regulations, copyright, laws, and trademarks can all be extremely confusing to beginners. Thankfully, you will know where to start!

When choosing a blog name, *protect it with a trademark registration*:

- Pick a great name by avoiding ones that are too descriptive and only describe what your blog is about in a bland way, such as *"Jane's Baking Tips"*.

- Better name choices are suggestive instead, such as *"Hummingbird High"*.

- Ensure it is unique and that your name is not already being used by another business. Just Google search your name.

Utilize the correct website documents, disclosures, and disclaimers:

- All blogs online are required to have a <u>privacy policy</u> if you plan on collecting any kind of personal information, even if you are just asking for an email. You should link it inside the website footer. (<u>Here is my favorite example template.</u>)

Get strong contracts in place with vendors, contractors, collaborators, and sponsors:

- When you are trading anything, such as blog posts, your time, or services for any type of money, you should place that agreement in writing. If you are just starting out, you can create your own contracts. They should include:

  - Write a list of products and/or services in detail
  - Itemize each task and the total cost
  - Write out payment deadlines
  - Include a refund policy, if necessary

o   How either side of the partnership can end the agreement
o   Who will own trademarks or copyrights in things being created

Add protection to your blog with copyrights:

According to copyright laws, you automatically own the rights to everything you create on your blog, from text, graphics, music, photos, videos, and everything in-between.

While adding this to your website is not required, I highly suggest claiming copyright and enforcing it on your blog. The notice should have a ©, the year content was curated, and your name (if you are the owner).

Ensure you use other creator's content the correct way:

If you didn't create a piece of content yourself, you will need to ask permission to use it first unless it is otherwise specified.

- Do you need an image? I suggest Unsplash.com or try out other royalty-free or creative commons license images.

SSL Certificate

As a beginning blogger, you may or may not have heard about SSL certificates and how to move your website's domain from http:// to the more secure https:// version. It sounds super techy, but it is very crucial. SSL certificates will drastically affect your blog's performance and security.

SSL stands for *secure sockets layer* and is the technology that is used to created encrypted links between your browser and web server. This lets data pass between the two and allows it to remain private.

Blog Disclosure

If you plan to ever make money from placing affiliate links on your blog, then you are required by the FTC (Federal Trade Commission) to add a disclosure. This is just as important as the required privacy policy. This helps you to build transparency between you and your readers.

Furthermore, you are required to add this disclosure to the very top of every piece of written content that is sponsored or that include affiliate links. Here is the one I use for all my blog posts:

"DISCLOSURE: THIS POST MAY CONTAIN AFFILIATE LINKS, WHICH MEANS WE MAY RECEIVE A COMMISSION IF YOU CLICK A LINK AND PURCHASE SOMETHING. PLEASE CHECK OUT OUR DISCLOSURE POLICY FOR MORE DETAILS."

Email List Building

I still regret not starting an email list building strategy right from the beginning when I ventured into the world of blogging. If you don't have an email list, you are essentially shooting yourself in the foot. You lose interested people that you can sell your products and/or services to! They are crucial to your blog's success.

- Find an email service provider that can help you manage and grow your list over time, such as ConvertKit.

- To those that are not so tech-savvy (a.k.a. ME when I started), here is a great article that thoroughly goes into detail on step-by-step how to set up your email auto-responder to help build a massive email list.

Email Freebies to Grow Your Subscriber List

Subscriber lists are great methods to get your readers to return to your blog time and time again. Many bloggers promote what they have to offer through newsletters that subscribers get. This helps you to earn more money!

There are many awesome ways to get brand-new subscribers that are easy to implement that you can offer as "freebies." Let's be real; *everyone* loves free stuff!

The easiest method to provide your fans with your freebies is with a plugin that automates everything for you. Talk about saving a headache. I personally use a premium plugin called ConvertPlus, but there are free plugins out there too. I set it up so that when people subscribe to my newsletter, they will receive an email with a free guide attached.

Examples of good freebies:

- eBooks and PDFs
- Guides and tutorials
- Design templates
- Photo presets and filters
- Schedules and calendars
- Checklists
- Free consultations
- Cheat sheets
- Premium content
- Sample products

How to Create a Freebie

Creating blog freebies to send to your subscribers is s superb skill that will be tremendously valuable as you escalate your blog's success.

1. Listen to what your readers want. Ask what they need and what tools they desire to help them resolve issues. Create a Facebook or blog poll!

2. Analyze what your readers are trying to tell you. I personally utilize Google Forms since it is free and easy to use. There is a button that converts the answers right into a spreadsheet for you!

3. Brainstorm opt-in freebie ideas. Sit with the data you have collected and interpret what it says. Then, think of at least 5 ideas for offers. Write them down and look at your data. What fits in the best with your reader's needs?

4. Pick a format to create your freebie on. It could be:

    - Video series
    - Mini-course
    - Planner
    - Checklist
    - Resource
    - Guide(s)
    - Free reports
    - Etc., also any of the above listed in the last section

5. Make your freebie look presentable and eye-catching. I would recommend going to paid stock photo websites such as Posh Shock or Haute Chocolate because you will receive

amazing looking photos. Tight on cash? Then I recommend Unsplash!

6. Deliver it automatically to your readers with the use of an email provider. You want a good company that will deliver your freebies straight into the inboxes of your readers.

7. Attract eyes to your newly created freebie by:

    o Promoting on Facebook groups
    o Creating an opt-in landing page
    o Pinning to Pinterest
    o Upgrade your blog's content
    o Adding to the end of your content
    o Sharing on multiple social media platforms
    o Asking other bloggers like you to share it
    o Guest post to other blogs!

As you can imagine, creating a great freebie that people will *want* to opt-in for takes a lot of work and some practice to get it done right. But make sure you are having fun and use your creativity too.

Your First Few Posts

Your blog essentially begins when you publish your very first post. This can be nerve-racking, as you can be fearful and confused. Instead of becoming overwhelmed right from the start, you simply need a plan of action to keep you on course to success.

- You need ideas, and I mean a TON of ideas; not just for this first post but for your future posts too. Stop what you are doing right now and go to Google Docs or somewhere on your computer and create a file for your notes and ideas that come to mind.

- Of course, to help you along, I will grant you a few ideas to get your juices flowing. (Go ahead and use these as well! Don't be afraid to utilize them for blog posts of your own.)

  First Blog Post Ideas...

- Create your ultimate guide post on the topic you know better than anything else. Be sure to link to other websites in your niche and notify them when you publish your post.

- Do some research in the area you feel a passion for.

- Share some statistics and figures: people love posts with data.

- Dispel some myths in an area and match them against facts.

- Create a list of inspiring quotes relevant to your niche.

- Describe in detail your process of creating something.

- Tell about other tactics you used to achieve results.

- Make a list of tactics used by other authoritative bloggers on some specific topic.

- Create some templates that will save your visitors' time.

- Tell how to make money in your niche.

- How to do something better and faster.

- Describe the most common problem your target audience faces and suggest a way of solving it.

- Remember what inspires you and create an inspirational post.

- Are holidays around the corner? Write what you're planning to do. Make a gift to your users.

- Reveal some truth: what is behind the curtain covering your work.

Images for Sharing

Yes, you have heard a few things already about blog post images, but for good reason; they are a monumental piece of every post you publish on your blog and you should not skimp out on quality.

2010 was a long time ago and there are many websites now where you do not have to pay for quality images. Here are a few free image sites that I personally use:

- Stocksnap.io
- Pexels
- Unsplash
- Burst
- Reshot
- Pixabay
- FoodiesFeed
- Gratisography
- Freestocks.org
- Picography

- MMT Stock
- Picjumbo
- Kaboom Pics
- SkitterPhoto
- Life of Pix
- Little Visuals
- Death to Stock Photos
- New Old Stock
- Jay Mantri
- Epicantus
- ShotStash

Most of the free stock image websites just require you to give credit where credit is due when you are using photos. Remember, photographers are hard at work creating photos that are free for bloggers like us to use; give them credit for their bomb photos!

If you are too wary of free stock photo websites, then by all means, here are a few paid stock websites that also have amazing photos for a small price:

- StoryBlocks
- iStock
- Adobe Stock
- Haute Stock
- Oh Tilly Styled Stock Photography
- Shutterstock
- 123rf
- Kate Max Stock
- Posh Stock

Photography Rules for Blogging

- Never use images on your blog that you did not get permission for or download from a free stock website.

- Don't take images from Google and use them on your blog. This is illegal, and you can get yourself into some troubled waters.

- Make sure you take the time to read the fine print when you receive stock images and know how you may need to attribute those photos.

Getting Readers to Share Your Content

As a blogger, it is not enough to just create amazing content, but you must reach your target audience. There is a ton of competition out there your content has to compete against to get the right people's attention, and it is very easy to get lost in the online crowd.

So, how in the world do you stand out amongst all that noise? First, ensure you are creating content that is relevant to the wants and needs of your audience. It should give them value, be informative as well as entertaining to read.

While sharing to Facebook is very powerful, there are other creative ways that you can get your fans to share your content on their social media platforms, which will help you triple your traffic:

- *Submit your content in a variety of places*, not just on the popular social media platforms. I encourage you to use lesser known websites such as Newsvine, StumbleUpon, Chime.in, and Reddit. People browse these sites daily looking for great new content to discover and share with their friends.

- *Become involved in a super-niche community* by following similar blogs, forums, and message board where like-minded people get together in your niche. There are even Facebook groups and pages dedicated to niche communities. These communities are valuable assets because it will help you attain new influencers and readers quickly.

- *Create previews of your content on various channels.* The more platforms you use, the better you are to test and get a taste of your readers and how they react and share your content. While Vine is no longer a thing in 2018, a small video that features links on your blog is more attractive to many people than just simply reading it, for instance. Post to Pinterest, upload to Instagram, create an overview on SlideShare. The possibilities are quite endless.

- If you are on a tight budget and unable to afford Google and Facebook ads, you can take part in *ad swapping.* This is essentially just an exchange between two publishers where they swap impressions and ads on one another's websites to help gain a stronger following.

- Become an active member on answer question websites such as LinkedIn, Quora, and HARO (Help A Writer Out).

Set up Social Media for Your Blog

Unless you have been living under a rock, we all know the power of social media and what it is capable of to helping those build their presence and businesses online. A huge part of a successful blog that will eventually earn you passive income is creating a social media strategy and consistently sticking to it.

While you do not need to necessarily use every single social media platform I am listing below, it is a good idea to at least pick ONE to start out with. Once you can consistently create content that attracts attention on one platform, you can move your expertise to another platform and so on.

- Facebook
- Instagram
- Twitter
- Pinterest
- Many, MANY more

So, how does one go about choosing the right platforms that will work best for their blog's content? Don't worry, I know how easy it can be to get overwhelmed with all the options out there.

I recommend you choose a primary and a secondary network to start out with. Your primary social media network is what you will spend the majority of your time on promoting your blog and its content.

Ask yourself these questions to choose the proper platforms:

1. What platform is your audience likely to engage with your content the most?

2. What platforms do you like to personally use and can see yourself having the most fun on?

Social Media Goals:

- Be social! Truly take the opportunities to connect with your target audience

- Share content that is valuable and entertaining

- Build up your assets and focus your efforts on getting as many people that connect with you on social media to subscribe to your mailing list. You OWN your email list, even when algorithms on social media channels change

The nitty-gritty of creating a website and bomb content is not so bad, right? Yes, it can be a lot of hard work learning the ropes and producing content that attracts people attention to read and follow you but remember that you need to have fun during this process too!

Don't be so hard on yourself; be patient and in time you will learn many of the ins and outs that will help your blog become successful in no time at all.

Chapter 5: Crafting the Perfect Post

Now that you have learned about the basic details and the techy aspects that go into getting your blog to run properly, become legal, and attract your target audience, it is time to learn how to write posts that are valuable, informative, and entertaining. Crafting the perfect post is a *must* in any blogger's world.

Making Your Content Scannable

Every single one of us "scans" content when we read it. People who read things online are searching for information to answer their questions or help solve their problems, which means they move through content quickly. This is why creating 'scannable' content is a necessity for any blogger to really hold the attention of your readers and influence them with what you have to say.

Here are some great ways to make all your blog posts scannable:

- *Use sections and subheadings* to break up your longer articles. I suggest breaking long-form content into at least 3 to 5 key points of sections.

- *Use white space* to help your readers' eyes focus on the copy and images on their screens.

- *Keep it short, sweet, and to the point*; this allows your message to flow much more efficiently and lets readers transition from one point to the next with ease.

- Create lists and bullet points, especially when you are presenting readers with many series of key points. This also breaks up 'straight-line copy' which can be hard to scan through.

- Limit your ideas to just one per paragraph. This allows you to break up your content into very easy-to-read chunks.

- Incorporate visuals such as photos and videos into your content. These are very powerful tools and amplify your content, as well as help break up the wording as well.

- Highlight key words and sentences with bolding to help emphasize crucial sentences or phrases within your text.

Adding Images to Content

Readers from all around the globe appreciate content that is made up of short sentences, has smaller paragraphs and plenty of white space. Instead of just using white space to break up chunks of content, however, using images is a great way to add visual appeal to your text.

To get the most out of adding images into your copy, here are some tips:

- Use a consistent sizing for your photos by resizing or cropping them. This makes your content look more coherent and consistent.

- Ensure that your photos are relevant to what your content is about. Obviously, if you are talking about cooking you don't need to add a photo of a tiger. Just make sure there are plenty of variety and colors in your photos as well.

- Make sure that you are getting high-quality images to add to your content. A huge killer of success is using images that are blurry.

- When you are fishing for images online, especially if you are gunning for quality shots, you will likely be using photos released to you by a *creative commons license*. This means that those images are free and okay to use, depending on where and what they are being used for.

- As you create content, you will likely find a screenshot or two to be necessary to ensure you get your idea across to your readers. I suggest using the *Awesome Screenshot for Chrome tool*; you can add text, circles, arrows, and more to really emphasize your point(s).

Be Clear with What You Write About

I am sure you have come across certain posts that just ramble on and on and never quite get to the point; aren't those *annoying*? The biggest issue that some bloggers have is writing with clarity and sticking to the ideas they are attempting to get across to their readers via text.

Creating clear and concise content of any kind is a lot like planning your route to a destination you have never been to before.

While you may have the best of intentions as a writer, writing with a lack of clarity can happen to the best of us, trust me! Here are some tips that I have learned to write simpler, clearer messages that persuade readers:

- *Clarify your content's destination and then choose the shortest route.* What do I mean by this? Well, when I first started out blogging, I would get an idea in my head and just start writing it out. Freewriting works well for some people, but for me, it complicated my blogging process. Therefore, now I create a plan for what I am writing about before I begin:

- o   Jot down the purpose of your post
- o   Create a list of what you want to include
- o   Review and narrow that list down
- o   Review your overall purpose and short list that content. Ensure that your post delivers on the promise you gave your readers.

- *Set up "signs" at each junction* so your readers don't become lost in the content. Your visitors should know what the content is about right when they arrive. This helps them maintain interest in your content and keeps them engaged enough to stay.

  - o   Use clear button copy text
  - o   Remind readers why they should be interested in buying what you have to offer
  - o   Remind readers why they should keep on reading

- Avoid the use of vague "route" descriptions. Your writing should not only be understandable but concrete as well. Abstract text can leave your readers feeling lost, while vivid language can make a more memorable message that they will remember:

  - o   Avoid using abstract terms and generic descriptions
  - o   Add in examples that will help beef up your text, such as mini-stories, case studies, etc.
  - o   Use metaphors

- "Dumb down" your choice of words. Tell me which one below you would rather go to:

  - A giant sphere that shines full of hot gas that compromises hydrogen, carbon, oxygen, helium, and nitrogen
  - A sunny beach

If you are like any other normal person I know, you would go to the latter,

right? Difficult words just make readers stumble through your posts.

Simple words and shorter sentences communicate your message easier.

Creating a Conversational Tone for Reading

How many times have you skimmed through a marketing email and automatically deleted it? I am sure you are familiar with that cringy feeling that marketing copy gives us.

The thing is, many bloggers fail to realize that their readers, no matter what niche you are in, crave connection with other people. When we read content that is in a more conversational tone, we naturally feel more connected to the blogger themselves. Because of this, your readers will want to get to know you and over time begin to like and appreciate your content.

Bloggers are content marketers and our goal is to get readers to like and trust us so that we can eventually market our products and services to them.

Here are a few ways to ensure that you are writing in a tastefully conversational way:

- Stop trying to write to *everyone*. Imagine your biggest fan; perhaps they frequently reply to emails and praise you with questions. They are your friend, even if you have never met them in the flesh. Conversational tones in writing emphasize that you are addressing each and every reader personally.

- Don't just write with the goal to impress people, for they will sniff you out quickly. Skip the nonsense and create specific content. You should always try to write to engage and to help!

- Create a two-way conversation in your blog posts. Even though you cannot physically see your readers on the other end, they are still there are the other end of the conversation. Edit sentences with "I" and "we" and make them more beneficial for your readers.

- Add some of your own unique personality. Why do you enjoy chatting with your favorite co-workers? Simple, because you like hearing and sharing stories with them, right? The same goes for your blogging tone. If you only talk about your expertise on a topic, it creates one-dimensional content. But, if you inject your personality into it, you share your mistakes, including personal anecdotes, etc.

- Engage your audience with questions included in your content. Questions are powerfully engaging and help to persuade readers.

- Embrace your voice's power; in today's world, more and more of us crave human connections instead of meaningless likes and non-stop pixels. Act as if you are brewing some tea and slicing some cake for your readers. Doesn't that sound like a perfect scenario to have a cozy one-on-one chat?

- If you are a grammar Nazi, like I used to be, you actually lose some readers. Why? Because no one likes to drink coffee with their high school English teacher. While you should not misspell things and create mumbled content, give yourself permission to break through the rules occasionally:

  o   Utilize "broken sentences" to add clarity
  o   Start sentences with "or", "but", or "and"
  o   Create paragraphs containing just one sentence to stress important points
  o   Feel free to occasionally use "uhm" and other human interactions such as "duh", "phew", and "ouch" in your text as well. Remember, the more connection you create, the more readers you will have.

Helpful Links

Being a blogger for almost a decade now, I have been right in the middle of the debate when it comes to linking out to other websites in your content. Many believe that it can harm their blogs reputation, damage search engine ranking, and cost them in the page ranks.

Well, in my humble opinion, their concerns are unfounded. Linking to other websites is a very common practice in the world of blogging, especially when you link to repeatable and likable websites.

There are *better* reasons why you, especially as a beginning blogger, should take the time to link out to other websites in your content:

- When you link to another piece of content that is valuable and helpful to your readers, it is likely that those that find your link will head straight back to your blog to take a gander around.

- Even if you are an amazing website builder, you will never be able to please and be everything for everyone, no matter how much content you pump out onto your blog. Linking to other websites allows you to leverage the internet and create a scalable path to your site's experience to make the best even better.

- Algorithmically, search engines will reward your website by linking to other reputable websites. Search engines put trust and value into efforts that yield in better results for readers and bloggers alike.

- When you link out, you are incentivizing the process of other bloggers or website owners to link back to you as well. It is a happy, positive cycle.

- Linking to other websites encourages contribution that is positive in nature

Crafting Emails to Ask for Links

Requesting blogs and websites to link back to your blog is more of an art than it is a science, especially if you are trying to get links from authority websites. When you are thinking about what to send in your link request, there are two factors to consider:

1. AIDA, or Attention, Interest, Desire, Action)

    a. You want to stand out from other people sending link requests:
        i. Use your contact's real name
        ii. Be creative and don't be boring in your email
        iii. Use the subject line and closing paragraph to your advantage

    b. You want the person you are requesting links from to read through the meat of your email while still gathering interest in linking back to your blog
        i. Focus on the benefits, not features of your blog
        ii. Give them recognition

    c. Once you capture their attention, you need to create the desire to act on your request
        i. Give them what they want – allow them to look over your freebies and other related materials
        ii. Make yourself available to them and allow them to feel special
        iii. Reinforce they reason why you contacted them in the first place by remembering to summarize the pros of linking back to you

    d. Don't give them time to think; instead, give them a code they can easily copy and paste into their content to make linking to your content a no-brainer

2. WIIFM, or What's in it for Me?

    a. Does that website provide resources that will bring value to your readers?
    b. Will their links achieve stronger associations to your blog?
    c. Are their links relevant to your niche?

Sample Link Request:

<Insert Badge or Anchor Text Optimized HTML Code>

As someone has an interest in <Category>, I've signed up to your site's <newsletter/rss> and look forward to learning more about your business. Please let me know if the above provides you with the information you need to review and consider our new section for linking. I'm available Monday to Friday 9am-5pm EST and can be contacted via telephone at my direct line (905) 420-1234 and also by my direct email <name@domain.com>.

Best wishes,

<Real Name>, <Client Name>

<Contact Details>

The Writing Process

One of the biggest fears that both beginning and experienced bloggers have is getting stuck in a rut when it comes to writing; writer's block is seriously the *worst*. That is why it is a good idea to have a writing process that works well for you in place to ensure that your brain won't become fried and your ambition won't fizzle out.

Before you start, you should create a writing template. This is a tool that will allow you to re-create similar blogging results time and time again. Each time you write, begin with this canvas, for it is a base for how you plan to craft your posts.

Here is an example of one I personally use:

Headline

- ❏ Surprise factor
- ❏ Clear benefit
- ❏ SEO Keyword

Hook and Big WHY for reader

Give the reader the feeling that if they keep reading they will overcome a challenge OR be able to add value to someone else by sharing.

- ❏ Connect with the reader personally
- ❏ Highlight a pain point of the reader
- ❏ Introduce 'Ace'
- ❏ Backed by stats or research

Table of Contents + Content Upgrade

If post is over 4,000 words

Body (List, Process, Step-by-Step, Framework)

- ❏ Anchors back to the 'Ace'
- ❏ Optimize for SEO keyword + long-tail phrases
- ❏ Sentences are short and easy for the reader to digest
- ❏ Sub-headings and dot points are used
- ❏ Informs the reader, before promoting the author
- ❏ Written to one person
- ❏ Topics are not over-explained, the reader only gets the information they need
- ❏ Helpful links are included where necessary (internal and external)
- ❏ Relevant images, informative screenshots and graphics are included

Conclusion

- ❏ Summarises key points of the post
- ❏ There is something clear the reader can put into action

Next, you will need to create a tangible version of your template, something that will help you to remind yourself of what makes your posts engaging and the best way to structure each section. I physically print off this checklist and tick things off as I write to ensure my content is top quality and formatted like the rest of my posts.

Now, you need to craft a writing process that you will be able to repeat time and time again. Document the steps you use to create a post, from brainstorming ideas to researching, etc. How long does each step in the process take? How can you better break down each step into smaller components?

You can download all these tools I personally use here.

Step One: Brainstorm and nail down an awesome headline

Once you have your templates and other writing organization tools set in place to keep your content on the right track, you need to perform brainstorming to figure out what you are going to write about.

I suggest that you never leave this to the last minute. Take time out of each day, even if it is just 5 minutes, to come up with ideas that you can write on. Write them down in a notebook or on an online calendar.

It is also important to be deliberate in the ideas you choose. What posts are you able to write that will complement your blog and its keywords?

Once you have got a good idea, it is time to think of 4 to 5 headline options for that post. Which headline do you think will grab the attention of more readers and get them interested in clicking your link?

Step Two: Research your idea

Now, you need to validate your idea and figure out what you will write about. Take your topic and head over to good ole Google. Click on any articles that turn up in your search, especially ones that catch your eye and sound intriguing. Paste those links into your writing template.

You don't need these articles right away, so don't spend too much time on this step. Take a maximum of 10 minutes to perform research.

Step Three: Create your blog structure and load it with content

This is the step where you will draw inspiration from the best of the best content on your chosen topic and decide on the best structure to please readers. It is time to read through the links you saved in the previous step.

Take it old school as you read through them all. Grab a pen and notepad and jot down key points and themes. As you do this, you will see a structure come together and after just a few edits, your chicken scratch will become a great structure to stand on.

Replace and generic headlines in your template with this new structure; it is time to get a little messy. Fill up your template and structure with the best content you located in your saved articles. Write or type this in a different color that stands out.

Copy and paste everything under each heading. The best content, as you will find out for yourself, will be interesting statistics and case studies that will beef up your content.

You can use this method to revisit older books, guest posts, and other content you have written in the past yourself; you should never let these things go to waste. This portion of the writing process should take you around half an hour.

Step Four: Write without Distractions

This is the step that many newbie bloggers panic on since the stress of crafting a great post becomes higher. Be wary, for this is when procrastination can set in when you should really be writing.

However, unlike many bloggers out there that are struggling, you are a step ahead because of the three previous steps! Pat yourself on the back! You have come up with a subject, researched it, and created a structured outline based on what you found. This will make writing much easier.

I refer to this step of the writing process as "baking" since we are essentially baking all the content you collected and turning it into an engaging blog post.

Sit down and set a timer for however long you want to write. I suggest intervals of 30 minutes and take a 5 minutes break in-between. Since you have broken your blog into sections, you can write these separately and use the timer that way as well.

As you write, do your very best to avoid anything else for that period of time. Don't add links or images or try to polish your post. Just allow your writing to flow so that you can capitalize on it later.

Step Five: Iron Out Kinks and Make Your Post Visually Engaging

Now that you have put some sweat and tears into pumping out content for your blog post, it is time to work out any kinks that may be hiding in your content. You need to read your post from start all the way to finish to help you spot any grammatical and spelling errors.

This is the time where you can add your links and fancy imaging into your post. Once you are happy with your content, copy and paste it into your blog publishing platform.

Step Six: SEO

Not so fast! Before you hit that "publish" button, you need to ensure that your blog content is optimized for search engines to find it and recommend it to readers.

Pick your blog's categories and tags and make sure to link to other internal posts on your blog that you have previously written and published. I also use the WordPress SEO by Yoast plugin to ensure that my keywords are adequately sprinkled throughout my post to help Google rank my content.

Guess what?! NOW you can hit publish! Yay!

Pro Tip: Don't Let Perfection Interfere with Writing

It is normal as you are writing to want your words to align perfectly with the vision you have in your mind. We all have an "inner editor" inside us. This is the voice we listen to as we craft our content, which forces us to pause and "think of a better word", for instance.

It can be very hard to concentrate and allow this voice not to ruin your writing flow. The truth is, you cannot edit and write at the same time, for it involves two very different parts of your brain. So, if you are constantly stopping to edit before you have your draft completed, you will find that the writing process takes much longer than it should, which makes you frustrated and difficult to find your creative voice.

Here are a few tips from me and other writing pros to help you get over that nagging inner writing voice:

- Remember, you will never learn to fly by reading about it, you must fly badly first. What do I mean? Just write poorly; it is OKAY. Remind yourself this isn't the final draft you will publish. In fact, what you are writing at that stage has yet to showcase your entire idea.

- Avoid premature feedback from those that are not in your natural audience; trust me, spare yourself this agony. Give yourself time to reflect on your writings and see where it goes. The more you write, you will find the deeper you get into the story or value you are trying to tell your readers.

- All art forms are created by imperfect people because no one is perfect.

- "Perfectionism" really means never completing a project.

- Writing is an art form, and no art is ever truly finished. Sometimes, as a writer, you need to learn to step away and come back to writing when you are in the right headspace.

Congrats! Now you have learned the details on how to craft engaging and highly valuable posts that your potential readers will want to read and engage in on your soon-to-be blog!

Chapter 6: Basics of Proper Advertising

Wow! You have absorbed a LOT of information about starting, creating, and maintaining your very own blog. I want to stop for a moment and thank you for sticking with me on this impactful journey of knowledge!

As you are well aware, without proper advertising and marketing, it can be challenging to get visitors, readers, and potential buyers to your blogging website to see what you have to offer. In this chapter, we will cover the basics of how to advertise your newly created blog efficiently and effectively!

How to Stop Being Overwhelmed by the Idea of Marketing

With all the different social media and marketing platforms out there online, it is no wonder why many bloggers get overwhelmed and too caught up in where to begin. However, after much delay myself when I first began blogging, I finally figured out that being in a constant overwhelming state was a *choice*.

There is no way any one person can tackle all aspects of their marketing plan all at one time; but if you do nothing, you are causing your business to fail from the start.

Here are the steps I took to cut through the overwhelm and start marketing my online business on a regular basis:

1. Just *stop* already! Step back, breathe, and take action to cut out all the "noise" that we are susceptible to online. What do you want to accomplish with your blog? What does your next step towards success look like to you? It is time to set concise goals so that you can create a plan to achieve success.

2. Once you have figured out your vision, you will need to establish goals that are realistic, specific, and measurable.

    a. Have a goal to land 5 new subscribers? Don't just say this to yourself. Instead, be more specific and say, "I will gain 5 new subscribers in the next 15 days." When you provide a timeline for yourself, you are more apt to do it and you can also measure your success.

3. Decide what marketing strategies will be the best to support the goals you have. If you want to attract 5 new subscribers, you need to market where your ideal readers are. Develop relations with those prospects so that you can learn what challenges them and build a rapport to help increase your visibility to them. Do this by leveraging your network that already exists and re-connect with past/current subscribers.

4. Create a simplistic plan that will help you to stay focused on only the strategies that will help you achieve your set goals. Instead of focusing on the next year, just tune into the next 3 months. You can get A LOT accomplished in 90 days. Map out the steps that you need to make your chosen strategy work for you. This will become your success roadmap!

5. Make it a priority to schedule time to work on your marketing plan. All that planning you just did will be pointless unless you pair it with action. You need to schedule time each day to work on your goals.

Pinterest for Business

If you really want people to discover your blog so that they can love and share your content, then you are missing out on a big opportunity to drive traffic to your website if you are not using Pinterest.

Pinterest is no longer for people just in the fitness, fashion, parenting, and cooking niches. In fact, Pinterest is the second strongest social media driver to my blog, which is also the case for a generous number of websites, from e-commerce to pets to education and MUCH MORE.

Pinterest currently has more than 250 million active users and gets 2 billion searches each month. This makes Pinterest a very powerful search engine all on its own! This means that you should really learn right from the beginning how to leverage Pinterest to your advantage to spread the word about your new blog by sharing your content on this platform.

The biggest lesson I learned about using Pinterest when I started using it as a traffic driver to my blog was that you get out what you put in. Here are a few crucial tips to help you achieve success with Pinterest:

- Make it as easy as possible for users to pin your blog posts. Essentially, other Pinterest users are helping you market your content, for *free.*

- Ensure that your pins have eye-catching, 'pinnable' images. Make sure that all your pins are 'Pinterest-friendly', which means that they should be nice and tall.

    o   600×900 pixels or longer

- o Easy to read (even on mobile)
- o Featuring a text overlay which gives Pinners an idea of what the source article will give them
- o Generally warm in tone, moderately bright, and do not feature faces.
- o Lifestyle images – allowing the person to see themselves in your Pin
- o Of professional quality
- o Subtly branded with a small logo or website URL

- Use the Social Warfare WordPress plugin so that you can display landscape-style images on your blog, but when readers go to pin it on their boards, the image will automatically turn into a perfect pinnable image! Even better, it also attaches your custom text to each pin description.

Learning How Pinterest Works

Pinterest, unlike other online platforms, is NOT a social network; rather, it is a platform to discover content *visually.*

Users of Pinterest utilize this platform to find and save inspiration in all kinds of niches. In essence, Pinterest is a solitary activity, which means you need to learn how you can appeal to this powerful group of potential readers/customers.

If you have never used Pinterest, I encourage you to sign up for an account and get a feel around to see how it functions for yourself. This will help you to become better equipped to promote your blog and its content more successfully.

Enabling 'Rich Pins'

Rich pins are those that pull data from your blog and show more details, such as the title, author, description, etc. The best thing about using rich pins is that you will always have a great description, no matter what a user chooses to add or remove.

Steps to enable rich pins on your WordPress blog:

1. Install the Yoast SEO plugin on WordPress
2. In WordPress, click on the "SEO" menu item in the sidebar.
3. Now click on "Dashboard."
4. Click on the Features tab and enable the "Advanced Settings Pages" feature.
5. Save and then refresh your browser window.
6. Back in the sidebar under SEO, you'll see a "Social" option. Click on that.
7. Click on the Facebook tab and check the "Add open graph metadata" box.
8. Click "Save Changes."
9. Apply for Pinterest Rich Pins.
   a. Enter the URL of a page or post from your site (any page should work).
   b. When you see the "Your Pin's been validated!" message, click on the "Apply now." link.
   c. Enter your domain name and choose "HTML tags" for your data format.
   d. Click "Apply Now."

Now, you have to be patient since it can take as much 1 to 2 weeks for your rich pins to be approved by the platform.

Using Good SEO on Pinterest

With Pinterest being a platform to discover, you will help yourself and your content get more exposure if you give Pinterest many clues as to what type of content you are pinning. Visual capabilities on Pinterest are awesome, but you may need to drop more hints so that users within your target audience can find you.

- Conduct keyword research to see what people search for on Pinterest. Simply type in words into the search bar and see what comes up

- Use your keywords the right way and be sure to use them:
    - In board descriptions
    - In board titles
    - In image names – when you save images to your blog, give them keyword-rich file names
    - In pin descriptions
    - In your blog post titles and URLs (you're already doing this, though!)
    - In your profile description
    - In your profile name

Writing Eye-Catching Pin Descriptions

Descriptions on pins inspire users that come across them to take action. Include a call to action in the click-through prompt and again when they have arrived on your landing page or website.

Make sure to keep all descriptions short and to the point and remember to sprinkle your keywords in too!

Pro Tip: Put More Life into Your Content with Multiple Pins

If you have some blog posts that have reacted well to being placed on Pinterest, you may want to breathe new life into those pins, creating a brand-new image and re-sharing it!

Also, if you have a blog post that is in long-form and easy to split up into multiple sections, then, by all means, take advantage of this and split them up into many images to pin onto your profile.

- For list posts, create two pictures for the entire post and then one image for each of those sections. You have now created more than one avenue for Pinterest users to find your content.

One Pinterest Board for All Blog Content

80% of the content you see when you hop onto Pinterest is actually pins that have been repinned. What does this mean for you? That any fresh content you put out can be a winner! This is why you should maintain just one board that houses all your blog's content, which makes it a one-of-a-kind board. This will become your most valuable board or asset on Pinterest.

Make sure to be creative and use a bit of SEO in your board titles as well. Branded searches are rare, but it is very possible that someone can come along searching for your business/blog on Pinterest, so it does make sense to include your blog name.

Group Boards

Also known as the collaborative board, group boards are those owned by just one pinner who invites other pinners to add pins to their board. The biggest advantage here is that all the pins show up on the feeds of those that are also in the group too.

I suggest using Pingroupie to help you find quality group boards so you don't spend too much time on it. When you find ones you like, simply find the owner, click their profile, follow, and click their website. Content them through their website and ask for an invitation.

Facebook Basics

There are many ways to promote your blog's content, but so many are quite time-consuming. Reaching out to fans and influencers, contacting about getting backlinks, etc. can really take away from your time.

However, Facebook is a platform that has now reached over 1 billion people and it is only increasing in popularity. Facebook is unique in that it has audience-targeting abilities, which allows bloggers to reach the right people almost every time.

I have had both great and terrible luck with Facebook since it is one of the most distracting platforms out there, it can be easy to get off task. Here are the steps I use to ensure that I captivate my target audience with my Facebook blog posts:

- First, the best way to start out for anyone promoting their blog content is using Facebook for *free*. Don't get carried away with paid ads and all that just yet. Post links to your blog's Facebook page if you have one.

- Boost your Facebook posts to promote your content to more people. You can set up a small budget, choose your audience and boost. The best time to do this is just one hour after publishing an article on your blog.

- Make sure you use headlines that captivate Facebook users. They won't click on your ad or post if you fail to do this. Also, be creative! I use different headlines for Facebook than what my article title is all the time to capture the attention of all the zombies mindlessly scrolling through their newsfeed.

- Use images that are designed well and avoid free stock photos from Google. I use the free site, Unsplash to create mine. **Pro tip: Use Canva.com to create social media images for *free.***

- Another huge part of becoming a successful blogger or business person in the online world is learning how to write copy that converts.

  - Ask questions to captivate people's attention.
  - Offer solutions to common problems.
  - Play on people's emotions and ignite curiosity.
  - Use clear calls to action to show the next step.
  - Use testimonials and facts to increase credibility.

- Make sure that you are targeting the correct audience on Facebook by figuring out who would be most interested in your articles. This can drastically affect your cost per click (CPC) traffic.

- Don't be fearful of using emojis in Facebook posts either; they add a pop of color and help you to distinguish what you are feeling or trying to convey to those on the platform.

Create a Facebook Page That Converts

A Facebook page dedicated to your blog and its content is another great avenue to use this popular social media platform to your advantage to get people to view your website.

First, it is perfectly fine to be logged into your personal account when you create a fan page. While some people set up a run-of-the-mill Facebook profile with their blog name, it is better to set it up as a fan page. This way, your readers can "like" your blog without having to add you as a friend first, which makes the page easier to control overall.

Here are step-by-step instructions to help you set up your first fan page for your blog:

1. Head to http://www.facebook.com/pages/create.php
2. Click on Brand or Product
3. When prompted to select a category, choose Website
4. Type in your blog's name under Category
5. Check the Facebook TOS and hit Get Started
6. Provide the basic information required of you
7. Upload a profile photo
8. Add your page to your Favorites
9. Explore your fan page settings and prompts

How to Grow Your Facebook Following

- Run Facebook ads
- Invite people to like your page
- Create content that is likely to go viral
- Host giveaways
- Add the "Facebook Likes Pop-up"
- Try out and use the Facebook Live feature

- Partner up with a social media influencer or someone with authority in your niche
- Utilize automation tools to boost your overall activity
- Add a "Facebook Like" widget to your WordPress blog
- Add social media links to other platforms to your website
- Email your list when you post new things, giveaways, live videos, etc.
- Create more video content to post
- Engage actively with your Facebook fan community
- Use hashtags wisely
- Offer coupons to those that like and follow your page

Facebook Groups

Facebook groups are more than all the rage when it comes to blogging; these places are where conversations are happening and helping bloggers dish out valuable content and create successful blogs. Essentially, Facebook groups are a fantastic way to grow your blog's following, which is why you should learn how to use them right out of the gate when you publish your blog.

The purpose of these groups is to bring together communities of people with the same interests. It allows followers to interact, connect, network, and share ideas with one another. It also allows people to ask questions, provide feedback, and ask for help, etc. Here is a list of Facebook groups for bloggers and entrepreneurs.

Facebook group tips for success:

- Be genuinely yourself
- Be constructive
- Don't just hit and run; provide value before hitting group members with your blog and affiliate links
- Play nice with others

- Follow the rules of the group
- Narrow the list of Facebook groups you want to join down to the essentials
- Size does matter; while large groups of 10,000+ are great, smaller groups give you the chance to really showcase your posts
- Minimize distractions and don't get too caught up on Facebook
- Be attentive to questions and things people comment on your content
- Take advantage of Promo days when admins allow those in the community to promote their links and blogs
- Optimize your personal Facebook account so that you can professionally interact with potential new readers and consumers.

Twitter Basics

I find Twitter to be an unusual but effective social media platform to promote my blog content on, for it provides me with insights on how to make my content even better in some ways! Here are some pro tips that I have personally acquired from my experience with using Twitter:

- Use Twitter Advanced Search to retrieve advanced search results, which is especially helpful for blog topics.

- Clean the Twitter feed with that advanced search tool by filtering through the people you follow. If you are lucky enough to have thousands of Twitter fans, it can become difficult to keep up with all of them. Narrow down your results and filter the folks you want to follow back.

- Keep track of those that mention your blog on Twitter. You can use that nifty advanced search tool for this too by looking for blog mentions of your blog's Twitter handle.

- Allow the <u>analytics</u> on Twitter to become your best friend. This is where all your metrics on this platform can give you the information on how your tweets are performing.

- Use paid Twitter promotions to get organic and targeted traffic to your blog's tweets. Promoted tweets are just like all the other tweets but with money behind it, they perform better.

- When you Tweet, get quadruple the traffic out there by pinning your tweets on Pinterest and vice versa!

- You can insert four images per tweet, which allows you to have 140 characters of text, tag people, and place four whole images, which can help with product reviews and so much more.

Instagram Basics

I absolutely LOVE Instagram both for personal use and business use to help promote my blog and keep my subscribers and fans up to date on what is happening and new events. If you are wanting to become a blogger in 2018, you should get yourself an Instagram dedicated to your blog like, yesterday.

Here are some tips I have learned with my years of experience with Instagram:

- Choose a great username. You want something professional yet catchy.

- Add a nice profile photo.
- Create a bullet-pointed bio that can provide links directly to your blog and inform users about what your blog is all about.
- Stick to your blog's niche. If you are a food blogger, then you obviously should be posting great food photography.
- Learn how to tell a good story and tell it through the posts on your account. Photos already tell a thousand words, use the right words to beef it up further.
- Use hashtags that are relevant to your post and niche.
- Geotag places you visit and discover.
- Follow, tag, and engage with others in your niche.
- Use the Instagram Slideshow feature to introduce your blog the right way on IG.
- Learn to embrace video content over photo content.
- Post consistently.
- Engage every single day with others; comment, like, follow.

Video Marketing Basics

One of the only thing bloggers (and the human race) want more than love and acceptance is more traffic to their websites. Okay, that might be overstating it, but marketers work their buns off to convert more traffic into sales.

Just a few years ago video marketing was rarely heard of online. But in 2019, it is said that 80% of the world's internet traffic will be from video marketing. Video is certainly not a fad but a trend that will be staying in the marketing world for years to come.

To get you up to par and into the video marketing game, here are some of the best video marketing practices to help you skyrocket your blog's traffic:

- Post a minimum once a month (the more the better).
- Establish a rhythm in your posting. This will prompt Search Engines to come back and check your channel. Adhere to the schedule you create.
- We recommend YouTube, but Vimeo will also do the trick.
- Keep it short – under five minutes for more in-depth videos, but sometimes all you need is 60 seconds and that's fine.
- Optimize the title and the video description with your targeted keywords
- Add tags and categories that are relevant to the video content.
- If you are using YouTube, make sure it is connected with your Google+ page or profile. Every time you upload a video it will automatically get added to the posts tab of your Google+ page or profile.
- Ensure there is a place on your website for your videos to live (category for the blog, stream on the home page or footer).
- Style your YouTube account to include your firm artwork, photos, updated description, custom URL, and links to your website and social media pages.
- Choose the best thumbnail for each video. You can verify your YouTube account to upload a custom thumbnail.
- Include a YouTube/Vimeo social media icon on your homepage.

Your videos need to be about current and popular topics, no matter what niche your blog/website is in. If you happen to have the means to interact with news when it happens, take full advantage of this. Make sure to always use topics that are relevant to create video content on.

Guest Posting

Guest posting was one of the best things I ever did to drive more traffic to my blog, gain many subscribers and rake in the sales. Guest posting is just like it sounds; you offer to create a post for someone else's blog or website and you will get a big whopping piece of their traffic.

Although I am unsure if guest posting has the benefits it once did 7 years ago, I believe it is still a good way to help build up your brand, increase traffic and get multiple links back to your blog.

Here are some guest post tips to help you get your blog's name out there:

- Guest post on websites where your target audience may hang out. Also, ensure the websites that you guest post for are of high-quality. You don't want to waste time creating awesome posts for crappy websites.

- Submit original content and avoid any duplicate content that might already be published on your blog.

- Write *very* well; in other words, these posts should be your *best* work.

- Follow the guidelines that the website owners have set in place. Submissions that fail to follow their guidelines scream that you are just writing for them for your own gain and that you didn't take any time to research what their website is about.

- Hold back the links back to your own sites and don't include your own affiliate links.

- Do your best to benefit not only your target readers but the readers of the blog you are guest posting for as well.

- Be a blog reader *first*; Comment and get involved with the communities of the blogs/websites you are interested guest posting for. You want to be an asset, not a nuisance to their audience.

- Don't be demanding when asking if you can submit your posts. Provide them with content that fits cohesively with their website, but also use your own voice as well.

- Make other website owners accept your guest posts with ease by:

  - Being kind, especially if your post is rejected.
  - Eliminate as many emails back and forth as possible. Try to answer your own questions. Be thorough and succinct. Keep your emails short and to the point.
  - Provide well-written, useful, on-topic content the blog owner can use "out of the box." Their readers will find it beneficial and you will feel proud to put out there.

Advertising is a huge chunk of the foundation that makes up a successful blog, website, or online business. When done correctly and strategically, social media platforms and other advertising methods can become assets to your business.

Chapter 7: Monetizing Your Blog

If you have made it to this chapter with success, then give yourself a congratulatory drink! Everyone starts their own blog with the dream to make money from it, but very few get there because they give up, fail to put in the work, or become lost in the truckloads of information out there online.

In this chapter, it is now time to get your money hands out and begin learning about ways to monetize your blog and actively work now so that you can eventually make a passive income later, which is the ultimate goal, right?

Affiliate Marketing for Bloggers

One of the best avenues I have personally found to monetize my own blog is to do affiliate marketing. Affiliate marketing is essentially promoting another company's products and when consumers buy from your links, you earn a commission.

The reason you want high-quality content when it comes to the point to monetize your blog is that the better the content, the more loyal readers you will have. The more loyal they are, the more they trust you, which makes them more apt to buy from your links. Your blog posts are great places to promote relevant products and services without compromising your integrity in any way.

Here are the quick four steps I talk about on my own blog to help beginning bloggers get starting with affiliate marketing:

Step 1: Pick relevant affiliate programs

When you use affiliate ads, you are paid per action, which means that when people click on those ads, register, or make a purchase, you get paid for these actions. This means you want very relevant ads that are cohesive with your content because it will be more likely that your readers will click them.

So, where should you start when choosing affiliate programs to work with? Well, a popular choice is with Amazon Associates since Amazon.com sells millions of products that can fit into the content of many bloggers in a variety of niches.

I highly suggest, however, that you also check out these affiliate clearinghouse websites that offer thousands of individual affiliate programs: ShareASale, LinkShare, and Commission Junction.

Step two: Consider an affiliate aggregator service

If you have topics on your blog that are more diverse, you may want to consider programs such as VigLink, which helps to automate access to 30,000+ affiliate programs and monetizes the links on your blog for you.

In addition, services like VigLink also insert new links where no affiliate links existed before in your content. Isn't that nifty? Talk about a time-saver! These websites life revenue from affiliate sales by more than 90%, which is definitely worth looking into.

Step three: Create content that helps you sell

I am sure you have read numerous blog posts where it was apparent that the blogger wrote the review of a product or service with affiliate marketing in mind. This is great, as long as you do it correctly without being overly spammy.

Blogs are so powerful when it comes to the world of affiliate marketing because of how easy it is to aggregate loyal fans, especially when it comes to niche topics. This gives bloggers plenty of authority to make recommendations and provide direct links to the products and/or services they recommend.

Instead of littering your content with spam-like junk, however, you should view affiliate links as additional resources to complement what you write. For instance, don't just like your favorite books with links; write detailed reviews of each one, explaining why they are your favorites and why your readers should buy them to read.

Step four: Add affiliate links to your blog the right way

When you add affiliate links to your blog, ensure that you maintain a good balance between user experience and monetization. The best way to do this is to keep the majority of your content free of ads and links, in other words, keep the bulk of your content totally free of ads.

Instead, a good practice for all bloggers is to dedicate 5 to 10 pages of awesome affiliate promotions and link them in the sidebar, foot, or other places where they will receive visibility. Then, keep the rest of your website ad-free. You don't need to monetize every page but remember that all pages can be a gateway to monetization.

Potential Earning with Affiliate Marketing

Ah, the question that almost everyone who is interested in making an income online has Googled; how much money can one make with affiliate marketing?

The truth is, there are five essential levels in the affiliate marketing realm when it comes to finally make some green with your efforts:

- Apprentice, where you lose money
- Low level, where you are making $0 to $300 per day
- Intermediate, where you make $300 to $3,000 per day
- High Level, where you make any number above $3,000 per day
- Extraordinaire, where you are making $10,000 or more per day

The numbers above are what affiliates in the five levels make in profit, not revenue. A huge rule of thumb is this saying about affiliate marketing; *"Profit is sanity, revenue is vanity."*

Affiliate marketing can be somewhat of a gambling game; intermediate affiliates can drop a level after losing on a campaign while the newbies can turn into the top dog overnight if they come across an unsaturated niche.

So, what is the *average* affiliate marketer earning? The median amount for great affiliates is between $81,000 to $120,000 per year, which is $221 to $328 per day give or take.

From an experienced affiliate marketer, I can say that what you can make with affiliate marketing heavily depends on the work you put in, as well as the amount of time you go to further your education in this industry.

Advertising Income for Bloggers

Advertising online revolves around three types of ads that bloggers can utilize to monetize their websites:

- Pay per action is where advertisers pay bloggers every time their ad is clicked, and an action is performed, or a purchase is made.

- Pay per impressions is where advertisers pay bloggers ads to appear on the blog's page.

- Pay per click is where advertisers pay bloggers every time people click on their ads.

Contextual ads are a type of pay per click ad that is delivered to the website based on where the ads can be displayed. The ads that pop up are typically relevant to the blog's content.

Text link ads are not posted relevant to the blog's topics but rather in specific posts. Text link brokers offer this advertising service to bloggers.

Impression-based ads pay bloggers depending on the number of times it appears on that blog.

Affiliate ads provide bloggers with a broad range of programs to choose from where they then provide links to products within their content. They are then paid when customers make a purchase from their unique link.

Direct ads give bloggers an option for visitors to post advertisements on their blog. Think of the banners you see on the sides of websites, that is what direct ads are. They are also referred to as "sponsors" of a blog.

Reviews are a great form of advertising on blogs. Many times, companies get in contact with blog owners and ask them to write reviews on their products, services, websites, etc. to get exposure. This can also be referred to as "paid per post."

Sponsored Posts are quite similar to review posts and are a form of native advertisement. They are made up of content that is in line with the niche of the blog and mentions very specific products in a natural context.

For instance, if you are writing about office supplies and mention a link in your text to an office supply vendor, this gives that vendor a great deal of exposure. The vendor then pays you for the mention. Traffic, audience, social media influence, backlinks, and other factors help to govern what you will be paid for sponsored advertisements.

See? Advertising your blog doesn't have to be as scary as the bigger gurus make it sound! In fact, once I got into the swing of things, advertising and getting involved with other companies to sponsor my content was a fun task that I enjoyed doing. It helps you to really get in touch with the right people that can assist you in skyrocketing your blog and its monetization potential.

Chapter 8: Promoting Your Blog

Just as important as advertising to the right people to gain exposure, you will need to put in some great effort to get the word of your new awesome blog out there for the millions of eyes to see. While there are thousands of other blogs already making bank and capturing the attention of your audience, it is not time to stand out amongst the crowd and get your voice heard! You can do this by putting efforts into promoting your content at this stage of the game.

Becoming an Affiliate

Affiliate marketing has become a very popular way to monetize websites and help even ordinary folks like you and me create an online business from home. One of the reasons it is widely known is because it is quite simple to become an affiliate. Here are a few quick steps to get you started!

- *Identify your blog's niche.* The internet is HUGE, and you want to make sure you have your niche down pat before finding affiliate programs that will compliment your content.

- *Choose affiliate programs* you want to partake in. There are many reputable websites out there. Put out feelers and sign up for an account! You need to be patient in this process until you find one that you truly like or multiple ones you want to use.

- *Create content* either around your affiliate offers (without being spammy) or place affiliate links within your existing and future content.

It is really that simple!

Understand the Affiliate Agreement

Affiliate marketing agreements are essentially contracts between a business and individuals/other companies who agree to promote the business in exchange for a commission. These agreements can be made for any type of business, for both corporations and sole proprietors.

As an affiliate for programs, you will have an agreement that will be required for you to sign. The two main parts are the contract itself and the monetary stipulations. Here are all the parts of an affiliate agreement:

- A section regarding nondisclosure and confidentiality of the proprietary agreement
- An indemnification clause that protects either party from actions caused by the other
- Any state or federal laws that would govern the transaction
- If and how the commission can be re-negotiated
- Licenses that are required by both the business and affiliate
- The procedure if either party ceases business operations
- The procedure in the event of a default
- The relationship of all parties
- The responsibilities of both the affiliate and the business
- The restrictions on the affiliate's use of promotional material
- The restrictions on the use of intellectual property
- The terms of the agreement
- The types of promotional and advertising that the affiliate can utilize
- Under which circumstances the agreement can be terminated

- What governing body will be used in the event of a lawsuit
- When and how the affiliate payments will be made
- Who has ownership over any intellectual property
- Who will own any necessary licenses?

Providing Value to Your Blogging Audience

One of the things I dislike about making money online is the other people that ruin it for those of us that are working our tails off to create content that is valuable to our readers and others that come across our blog. There are plenty of people that have the wrong mindset who are out there spamming their subscribers with links with no true effort to help people solve problems and make their lives easier.

Do me a favor and don't be one of those folks; realistically, it will get you nowhere and you will be wasting your time. Being spammy will only turn potential customers off and you will never make a dime.

It is the value that people receive from your blog that keep them coming back time and time again for years to come, even if you never write another piece of content and let your blog sit in the realm of the internet.

That being said, how does a blogger go about providing value to their readers?

Help your readers find solutions to issues they have. Your blog will receive thousands of first-time, one-time visitors because Google recommended your blog's content as a way to solve one of their problems. People come to these sites for a fix or ways to overcome what they are experiencing in life.

One of the questions I ask myself before sitting down to write another piece of content is, "How is this topic going to further benefit my readers?"

Another method that I use often is checking out the Google Analytics of your blog and seeing what pages your readers land on and stay on the longest. Look at bounce rates, time on your website, traffic sources, etc. This will help you to really grasp how to cater to your audience.

Show readers what is truly working for you and what isn't. I learned this the hard way at the beginning of my blogging career, but transparency is everything when you are trying to earn the trust of people you may never see in the flesh. The proof is indeed in the pudding!

So many bloggers are out there right now who are way too caught up in teaching things that they don't provide the value of what worked for them and what they didn't like in these processes.

Honesty is by far the best policy and it will show readers a true side of you and help them feel more connected to you as a human being, which will hopefully later translate to sales.

- Write case studies related to your success and failures
- Share details of reports, income, and progress
- Create honest reviews that are unbiased
- Tell stories to help engage with your audience

Repurpose content

Sometimes to create quality content you must truly become a master at seaming valuable intel from multiple blogs to get just what your readers are searching for. Also, you should take a walk down memory lane and see what old <u>articles you can repurpose</u> from your past publishing's.

Instead of just writing articles, create videos, eBooks, live-streams, slide presentations, etc. to relay new and improved information.

Make sure you are present

Even if you don't partake in any of the advice previously in this section, there is one thing you must do to ensure you are giving your audience the value they crave; *being there for them.*

There are many bloggers that preach about creating value, but when you look at the comment sections of their blog, they are nowhere to be seen. You should view unanswered questions as big ole opportunities for you to answer them and to ideas to create future content around.

If you want to engage in the meaning of true value to your readers, you must put yourself smack dab front and center in front of your following and be there for them as much as you can. Answer inquiries, assist them in finding solutions, etc.

Promoting on Social Media

These are the top ten ways that I myself promote my blog and its content on social media:

1. Include link(s) to your blog on every single one of your social media profiles
2. Schedule Tweets to help drive traffic. TweetDeck is easy to use.

3. Schedule your Facebook posts in advance to publish at high traffic times
4. Highlight content from your blog on Pinterest with eye-catching pins
5. Share your content on LinkedIn groups and on your LinkedIn profile
6. Promote your content in Google+ communities
7. Leverage chats on Twitter to help receive more blog visitors
8. Host Google Hangout chats with new and old visitors
9. Utilize forums to share your blog content and upcoming events
10. Create campaigns on your social media platforms to get your users excited for what is coming up next on your blog

Promote to Your Email List

The big collection of emails that you have from those that have subscribed to your blog is your email list. This is a powerful tool and can lead to campaigns that generate a nice chunk of revenue.

One of the worst things I did as a beginning blogger was not attempting to put efforts into growing my email list. So, if you are not already doing so, here are some tips to help it grow so you can reach more of your target audience, grow your blog, and get sales!

- Create awesome email content people *want* to read
- Encourage your subscribers to share your emails with others
- Add life to stale lists with an opt-on campaign
- Add links to your signatures for people to reach out to you
- Create new offers that will generate more leads
- Create freebies that people want
- Create content that is a "bonus" to your subscribers

- Promote contests online
- Promote lead generation offers on Twitter
- Promote your offers through Facebook that require their emails
- Ensure you use call-to-action buttons on your social media pages
- Use Pinterest as a way to promote your more visual content
- Add features for engagement on your YouTube channel if you have one
- Ask visitors to give you feedback
- Shorten your lead-capturing forms to make them even simpler
- Guest blog for other sites and add your call-to-action
- Add consumer reviews to your blog

Just like advertising, self-promotion of your blog is a necessity if you ever want it to see the true light of day and become a popular place for like-minded folks to hang out, read your content, buy your recommendations and spread the word!

Chapter 9: Becoming an Efficient Blogger

If you truly desire to be a successful blogger in this dog-eat-dog world, then you will need to make it a genuine portion of your every day and become just a bit obsessed with it.

There are many pieces of advice out there from those that finally figured out the ins and outs of blogging, but in this chapter, I am going to provide you with my own insight and what I have learned over the past decade of developing over fifty blogs and websites.

Habits of Effective Bloggers

First, you don't be afraid to spend a large chunk of your time at the beginning learning and observing from others. This is how I came across the traits that the top bloggers had to become successful, which are:

- To be successful in any career that involves writing, you must write *a lot*. Practice makes perfect so the more you write, the better you will become and more you will develop your own unique voice.

- If no one is going to be able to learn from your blog, what is the point of writing it? They come to you to learn and to fix issues, so you want to be clear and concise and eliminate fluff and banter.

- Bloggers with the highest successes don't live in a bubble; rather, they spend the time to get to know their target audience, what they do, where they are from, what they search for, etc. They take the time to get out of their head to figure out how to tailor their content to their prime audience.

- There is no way around it; if you are a beginner in the blogging world, you are going to naturally be on a huge learning curve. No worries, it is normal! But, even when you learn a lot about blogging, there will always be new things to absorb. The best bloggers realize this and have molded themselves to be lifelong learners.

- Focus and consistency are absolutely *key* in blogging; successful bloggers pick a topic and stick to it till the end. They also utilize consistent voices on these topics and when they go off-topic, they find ways to relay it back to the original topic at hand.

- It may take a while but eventually, you will discover what you want and where you want to go in your blogging career. Successful bloggers create their very own masterplan and do everything they can to stick to it.

- Persistence is another key to making a massive passive income with your blogging efforts. To be able to efficiently work from home, no matter what you do, you must be able to manage yourself and your time wisely.

Simple Steps for Effective Blogging

To become prosperous in the blogging world, you need to realize how important blogging is to digital marketing and how fast you can build your online presence when you stick to it and use the basics you have read about in this book. If you are able to produce awesome content quickly, know how to plan and use SEO and share your content, then you are on the right track.

For all the beginners, here are the steps I still use to this day to ensure that my blog and my online career stay the course I desire it to go:

Step one: Define your purpose for blogging

Yes, I suggest you ask yourself why you are blogging every single time you sit down to begin writing. Why did you create your blog? Perhaps you are:

- Blogging for money
- Blogging for leads
- Blogging for traffic

All these reasons are great!

- If you are blogging to create an income from home, then you may need to concentrate your efforts more on keywords that can help you generate money, or "buying keywords."

- If you are blogging to attract leads, you should be publishing posts that are detailed and bring insight to your readers into making a decision.

- If you are blogging for more traffic, you will need to blog more often and about topics/niches that are trending.

Step two: Conduct thorough research before you put pen to paper

The biggest time consumer for bloggers is writing content but before you dive into this, you should always research your topic. Use Google to search for your topic and its related keywords. What are other already writing about your topic?

Really take time here; analyze the first page results of your search, open websites and read through blogs. Are they similarities? Do you see any patterns? Your entire goal is to make your blog's content *better* than the rest so that you stand out from the crowd.

Step three: Choose your titles (wisely)

Now that you have a topic and have researched it, you will need to come up with a title that is eye-catching. You want it to be catchy and SEO friendly.

Decide on your keywords and type them in the search bar and see what related searches come up; this will help you tremendously in creating perfect titles for your posts.

Step four: Create an outline

With your title optimized, you can now craft an outline which is essentially your post's foundation. This will save you tons of time later and will help you keep the course to ensure your post stays on task.

Step five: Write an intro

Almost as important as a good title, the introduction to your blog posts is crucial to keep readers reading and to help the remainder of your content to flow nicely. Make your intro 2 to 3 sentences and explain what your post is about.

Step six: Post length

Size does matter when it comes to online content; longer posts just perform better in the search results and are much more likely to be shared. Look up similar articles in your niche and see how long other posts are and write in similar length.

Step seven: Use basic SEO

SEO is a crucial part of article writing and there is no reason you must be an expert. All you need is to go through the basic concepts during your writing process like we previously discussed. Here are the high points of good SEO practices:

- ALT tags for images
- Descriptions between 140-150 characters
- Fast loading pages
- H1 tag for the page title and H2, H3 tags for the headings
- Internal linking
- Mobile friendly content
- Set a Canonical URL for the page
- Structured Data implementation
- Titles less than 60 characters
- Well-formed permanent URLs

Step eight: Polish your work

Even when you finally finish your article, do not just click publish! Go back through and reread it at least once to ensure you have said everything you want, eliminate grammar and spelling errors, and structured your post to optimize reading.

Step nine: Get your blog post noticed

If no one reads, shares, or comments on your work, there is no real point to blogging. Get your content noticed by advertising, posting on social media, guest posting, distributing content, email marketing, and other methods you have learned about.

- Share the post on your social media business pages.
- Share the post (multiple times) on your personal social media pages.
- Post it on content discovery websites like inbound.org, growthhackers.com (there are similar websites for different niches).
- Advertise it on Facebook (use Facebook ads).
- Advertise it on twitter (use twitter promotion ads).
- Inform other fellow bloggers by email that you have published a new post.
- Send out a newsletter to your email list (if you don't have an email list, build one asap).

Step ten: Build consistency

Consistency is the way you will create the results you want from your blogging efforts. You can't publish five articles and hope to become famous and never do any more work. To increase your traffic, you must rinse and repeat everything you have learned to ensure that you grow your audience.

Becoming an efficient blogger takes practice, but if you are dedicated to becoming successful with it and make a passive income, then you are well on your way to fulfill your dream of a life full of freedom, passion, and fulfillment with blogging!

Conclusion

Thank you for making it through to the end of *Blogging for Beginners*!

I hope that the information in this book was not only informative but valuable, providing you with all the tools and knowledge you need to achieve your goals of creating and maintaining a successful and profitable blog.

A disclaimer: For all this information you have absorbed to work for you and help you to create a passive income, you will need to be ready to put in the work. This may mean working after your 9-5 job and picking up part-time work on the side to make ends meet and to help you create your online blogging business.

However, if you have a passion to provide valuable information about your interests and passions to the online world, all the while making a side income to help you achieve your dreams!

The next step? To take action, starting *today*. Nothing but procrastination and doubt is holding you back from researching niches, brainstorming a domain name, deciding on your target audience, and curate content!

The best advice I have for all you beginning bloggers out there is this; building a strong foundation of your first online business should be conducted in baby steps. If you fear failure, take it one step at a time:

- Day One: Look deeper inside yourself and write your thoughts down

- o   What are your passions? What drives you? What interests you? What could you talk about for hours at a time?

- Day Two: Pick a niche
  - o   Research potential audience, create your ideal reader, look closer at your readers' habits, conduct niche research

- Day Three: Domain and hosting
  - o   Create a unique but simple domain name, buy it and purchase hosting

- So on and so forth...

When you break down each crucial part of blog creation into baby steps, you will be more apt to stick to continuing to create it and maintain it successfully. I encourage you to write down the high points of this book and break them into sections that you believe you can accomplish in a day. This will fend off feeling overwhelmed and the desire to procrastinate.

The more passion and dedication you have to your piece of online real estate, the more desirable it will be to work on. With all the information you have just read, you are already on a great start to creating the passive income you have always wanted!

Finally, if you found this book useful in any way, a review on Amazon is always appreciated!

Description

The grind of the 9 to 5; it's what we are taught and encouraged to achieve. We spend an average of 14+ years of our youth becoming educated and spending thousands of dollars on our degrees. Then, we are thrown into the real world where the jobs we worked so hard to get are not what they are cracked up to be and we get stuck in a rut that is hard to dig ourselves out of.

Now, cue the internet. It's inevitable in 2018 and we have all seen the "too good to be true" financial opportunities that the World Wide Web offer. While the scams are being weeded out, there are many options out there to help you make another source of income. So, what path should you choose to make money online?

Yes, there are thousands of blogs and niche websites out there, but 2018 is the prime time to start building your piece of real estate online, adding value to the lives of everyday people, all the while creating a nice passive income for you and your family.

Don't quit that 9 to 5 job *just* yet, but this book will help you to see the light to the day that you can place your suit in storage and wear your pajamas to work!

In this book, you are going to learn about all the tools you need to build and maintain a successful job as a total beginner. Whether you are on the fence about the whole process of blogging or have been thinking about starting a blog but are unsure where to start, then this is the perfect book to begin your journey into the realm of blogging!

What you will learn:

- Prepping methods to ensure your blog has a solid foundation
- Detailed steps on how to create a blog
- Methods to successfully maintain your blog over time
- The ins and outs of website creation
- How to craft perfect blog posts and content
- Free and paid methods of advertising to attract traffic to your website
- Awesome methods to monetize your blog
- Unique ways to promote your blog to potential consumers
- The basics of products and how you can make a substantial income
- Tips and tricks to help you become an efficient and consistent blogger
- As well as much more!

Blogging doesn't have to be a frightening journey; in fact, creating your own blog or website is now easier than ever with all the wonderful tools online to ensure that if you are willing to put the work in, you will achieve success and begin seeing a passive income roll into your account.

So, what are you waiting for? Your blog is only a brainstorm and a click away from becoming a reality and beginning to earn you additional income, enough to even stick it to your boss in the future and live a life of freedom and fulfillment.